DMSO

The Responsible User's Guide

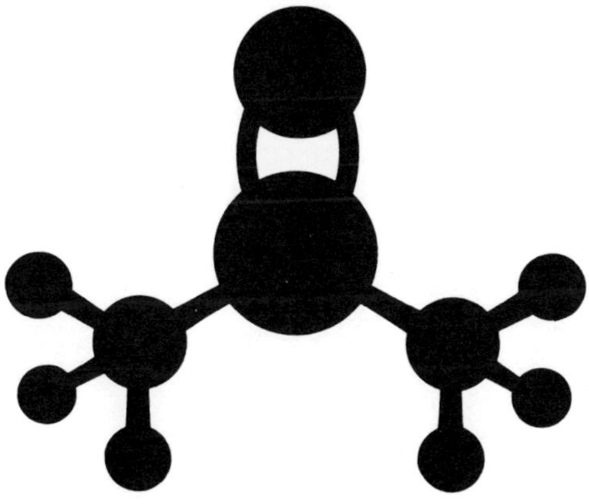

by Thomas Bristol

illustrations by Geof Sauncy

Dedication

The only safe depository of power in a democracy is in the people themselves. And, if the people fail to exercise their power with discretion, the answer is not to take the power from them (through control), but to educate their discretion.

Thomas Jefferson

ACKNOWLEDGMENTS

I am indebted for comments and suggestions from a number of physicians, researchers and friends who read all or part of earlier versions of these chapters, including Stanley W. Jacob, William J. Weaver, Suzanne Graham, Ken Doney, Frank and Barbara Weber, Bob Dernedde, Dick Raymond, Barbara Roberts, Susan Christ, and Henry Bristol.

Many of the quotations, tables and graphs, and much of the data, are either taken directly or modified from volumes 141 and 243, *Annals of the New York Academy of Sciences*. References to volume and page are entered as follows: (141:252).

Special thanks to Dick and Sandi Magedanz and Linda Snyder for their diligent work in typing and correcting the manuscript.

 For information address The DMSO News Service, Suite 103, 10149 S.W. Barbur Blvd., Portland, Oregon 97219.

ISBN: 0-940530-00-7

CONTENTS

Preface

The original concept for the design of this book was that it should be something like an expanded package insert, similar to those found in many prescriptive medications.

I had been involved, a number of years ago, in reviewing the scientific evidence on DMSO and writing the package insert that is now carried with RIMSO-50, the Research Industries Corporation DMSO product approved by the Food and Drug Administration. Before that, I had worked on the popularization of an anatomy in physiology text book for Practical Nursing students.

It seemed natural to combine the knowledge and skills acquired in each of these previous ventures to produce a popularized package insert for people who wanted to learn the practical basics about DMSO.

The need for such a book became clear soon after Dr. Bill Weaver, Frank Weber and I had decided to put together a regular newsletter about DMSO: **The DMSO Report**. The newsletter was written primarily for the biomedical professions - both practitioners and researchers, and for those concerned citizens committed to obtaining accurate, up-to-date information on DMSO.

Valuable as it is, the newsletter is not likely to fulfill the basic information needs of the current estimated 6 million regular and 22 million occasional DMSO users.

The aim in writing this book was not to promote the use of DMSO. In fact, to the contrary, many now casual users of DMSO may well have second thoughts. Despite its relatively low toxicity compared to other therapeutic agents, DMSO is nonetheless a powerful biological substance.

The principal aim is to educate those who have already chosen to use DMSO for medical purposes, and for those who may, independently, choose to do so in the future.

Secondarily, this book is a first attempt to provide an accurate source of information about DMSO for the professionals - physician, chiropractor, physical therapist, veterinarian, etc. As a result, the text is really written at two levels, one very popularized and the other slightly technical.

Specialized publications for biomedical professionals are currently (1982) in preparation for each area of established usefulness of DMSO. Send in the reader reply card or write to **The DMSO News Service**, Suite 103, 10149 S.W. Barbur Blvd., Portland, Oregon 97219, in order to receive notification of availability of these new materials.

As mentioned, the original concept here was to produce an expanded version of the package insert normally found in prescriptive pharmaceutical products. Consequently, heavy emphasis is given to the discussion of the possible side effects and adverse reactions - and what to do about them if they should occur. Special attention is given to the important question of possible eye toxicity. (There are still no documented cases, and it appears to be highly unlikely any will ever show up.)

Pharmaceutical package inserts in the past have been designed to be read only by biomedical professionals. The non-professional may, therefore, be a little disturbed to read the details of reported side effects with DMSO. In fact, compared to the listings of side effects and adverse reactions associated with most other prescriptive pharmaceuticals, DMSO is ranked as being uncommonly safe, and really rather difficult to abuse. Hopefully, the reader will discuss what he learns in this book with his physician. Only this way can our evaluative statements be independently confirmed.

Of particular interest will be a careful review of the most extensive human toxicity studies - the 14-day and 90-day studies carried out on prisoners at California State Prison in Vacaville, California.

Other related features include procedures for making a preliminary personal evaluation of possible dangers in using DMSO, and suggestions are made on how to reduce the risk of any long-term toxicity - if any should show up beyond the current 15 year negative data base.

A large number of people with diverse backgrounds were consulted during the preparation of the manuscript for this book. This led to two major developments. First, the package insert concept was too limited. A broader discussion of DMSO was essential to satisfy the curiosity and concerns of the DMSO users. Second, an outcome of the first, a question-answer format was adopted.

The questions answered were selected primarily on the basis of the preference expressed by actual DMSO users. Over 500 athletes and clinical patients were interviewed. Other texts, particularly the recent book, **DMSO: The True Story of a Remarkable Pain-Killing Drug**, by Barry Tarshis, should be seen as supplementary and complementary to this book. Nonetheless, a short history and simplified outline of the political and economic problems DMSO has experienced is included. The account here differs in some significant features from what Tarshis presents.

The final motivation for this book was a simple feeling of moral obligation. A conservative silence would have been easier. But there comes a certain point when one is called on to step forth, to take a stand.

Before proceeding, a judgment had to be made about the reality of the safety of DMSO in general. An extensive review of the literature and a 15 year familiarity with the top clinicians has convinced us on this point.

If the materials presented here are received by the public in a responsible manner, all our efforts will have been vindicated.

Thomas Bristol
Portland, Oregon
April, 1982

INTRODUCTION

The Responsibilities of Self-Medication

Modern scientific medicine during the first three-quarters of this century has tended to place greater responsibility for cure in the hands of the practitioner and less in the hands of the patient. More recently, it has become clear that in many areas, this trend has gone too far. The need for the patient to take more responsibility for his health is now universally acclaimed. This applies to maintaining an active, healthful life style, as well as increased responsibility in treatment and recuperation.

In order to take responsibility for one's own health care, it is necessary to be reasonably educated - at least about general do's and don't's.

The first principle of self-care is **never to rely on oneself for diagnosis**. Diagnosis must be kept separate from responsible self-medication and treatment.

We are all hopelessly biased in assessing our own conditions. Hopes, fears and external socio-economic pressures to minimize health problems continually invade our observations and reasoning and bias our judgment.

However, to withhold the tools and knowledge needed for self-medication and treatment - where self-directed therapy is feasible - based on fears of occasional, inappropriate self-diagnosis, would be unjustified and excessively paternalistic.

Every medical therapist - whether physician, chiropractor, homeopath or whatever - knows that medications are "helpers," not the sole cause of cure. Biomedical professionals are all taught that if they don't do anything to cause harm, most patients will eventually regain their health naturally. The body itself is the healer - with our cooperation.

This applies to DMSO virtually without reservation. Its therapeutic benefits all appear to result from its ability to release the natural healing and recovery processes which, for one reason or another, have become blocked or inhibited.

Responsible self-treatment requires that you respect your body's needs and cooperate with the healing process. Keep in mind that DMSO is only a helper. And its ability to help is limited. It cannot do everything. There may well be a better, more effective treatment for your condition. If so, you should use the more effective treatment, and not expect DMSO to do what it cannot do.

Another related problem is that some medications might help us to ignore or suppress signs of disease. This can be harmful in that it can contribute to a more severe outburst at a later time.

Because DMSO relieves pain, many clinicians have voiced concern that it might mask important early signs of serious problems - like cancer.

Stated more simply, there is a danger that your self-medication might interfere with responsible principles of diagnosis. But this applies to all medications. There is no obvious automatic solution. Be aware of the potential problem. **Consider stopping regular DMSO use for a few weeks each year to allow for adjustments and diagnostic tests**. Rely on your physician to pick up on the less obvious symptoms of more serious developing conditions. He is the experienced and well equipped diagnostician.

Once a condition has been properly diagnosed, a decision can be made as to whether DMSO or some other therapy is preferable. In all but the simplest and most familiar conditions, this is a decision that should be made in consultation with a biomedical professional. At least, one should ask the advice of another more experienced individual. For instance, in athletic injuries, the trainer or physical therapist will be up to date on the best therapies.

Considering the lack of health education among the populace, most persons may be best advised to rely completely on the supervision of a biomedical professional for their first few uses of DMSO. Once you have some experience and have received professional advice relevant to any unique personal conditions or possible drug interactions, then you may well be better prepared to take greater responsibility for your own care. A follow-up consultation to check on progress would also be wise.

Physicians and other biomedical professionals now spend almost one quarter of their time advising clients over the phone. This is very efficient. Don't be afraid to call for advice or help in making decisions.

In this book, we have dealt with the use of DMSO for a very limited number of conditions. Only those conditions are discussed that are reasonably within the competence range of the non-professional.

Nowhere do we consider intravenous administration of DMSO. Nowhere do we consider the injection of DMSO into a muscle or joint.

There are dangers with these routes of administration that cannot be fully grasped without extensive special education. This is the realm of responsibility of the biomedical professional.

The scientific evidence could be cited to argue for other applications. But self-treatment is not feasible in many cases. In a few instances, we decided that caution should prevail in this edition. Later editions will likely cover more.

We are also aware that there are situations where an injection of 20% DMSO into the joint may help to get on top of an otherwise difficult case. Less commonly, repeated injections may be appropriate. There is evidence that intravenous DMSO may be extremely helpful in certain conditions.

An important, developing attitude to DMSO among experienced professionals is that it is best thought of as an adjunct therapy. An adjunct therapy is one that works with other therapies, either to improve their effectiveness or by itself to provide some limited symptomatic relief.

Leaders in the field are attempting to remove the idea that DMSO, by itself, is a cure for anything - let alone a cure for everything (panacea). All this will better help DMSO to find its proper place in the modern therapeutic complex.

The information contained in this book is not intended or expected to take the place of one-to-one dialogue between patient and physician. However, it is hoped that it can serve to augment patient teaching strategies. Patients have the right to know important information about drugs they purchase and administer to themselves or to their families and children.

The information herein provided has been carefully reviewed for appropriateness, accuracy, and currency. We have tried to keep the reading level such that most readers can comprehend most of the words.

The DMSO News Service

The DMSO News Service was conceived by three individuals, each of whom has been close to the center of DMSO research and development for over a decade. The need for a single, credible source of information on DMSO had grown, along with new research findings and public interest. The traditional science journalists working for the mass media, newspapers and television, did not have the time to read a significant portion of the 3500 research papers on DMSO relevant to its therapeutic uses. A group of people with a broad background in the DMSO literature was essential.

Integrating large amounts of research literature on DMSO was not a new experience. As a team, we composed the first successful New Drug Application (NDA) on DMSO to the Food and Drug Administration. This required a comprehensive review of all research literature involving DMSO. Acceptance of that NDA made DMSO available for the first time as a prescriptive drug for interstitial cystitis.

It was appropriate we three should put together the first publication dedicated exclusively to general news and information on DMSO: **The DMSO Report**. This eight page newsletter is published ten times a year by The DMSO News Service; ISSN-0275-0648X.

The publisher/science editor, Thomas Bristol, has already begun a career in consulting on research policy with Tektronix and Oregon Graduate Center, and in scientific communication, editing two text books on human anatomy and physiology. A graduate of the University of California at Berkeley, he will complete his Ph.D. in the History of Methodology of Modern Science through University College London, England in 1982.

William Weaver, Ph.D., is an experimental pathologist, well-versed in the biological actions of DMSO at the cellular level. He has worked in both the academic and industrial settings on research and development of DMSO.

Frank Weber has a Master's degree in biology and has been involved in DMSO research under various investigators since 1969. His hands-on experimental experience is especially valuable in his role as investigative reporter. Frank also worked in the commercial sector on the chemical and pharmaceutical studies that define medical grade DMSO and standardized its analysis.

The DMSO Report

Suite 103, 10149 S.W. Barbur Blvd.
Portland, OR 97219

If you would like to receive the newsletter, *The DMSO Report*, ten times per year, place your order by calling our toll-free number 800-547-9755 (inside Oregon 246-1212). Or write to *The DMSO Report*, Suite 103, 10149 S.W. Barbur Blvd., Portland, Oregon 97219.

The cost is $49 per year. It is this high because we are a totally self-supporting scientific publication and accept no advertisements. You can still become a Charter Subscriber by placing your order before the end of 1982, and you will receive all back issues, absolutely FREE.

The first ten issues — Volume One — can now be purchased separately, bound, for $15.

The Original Concept and Policy

Dimethyl sulfoxide promises important therapeutic benefits in a wide range of unrelated disease and medical conditions. Because DMSO's biological actions are so varied, research data and clinical reports come from diverse, uncoordinated sources. A professional newsletter proves the ideal medium to report these data in one reliable source. Knowledge of the actions and benefits in one area may be essential to understand what occurs in other areas. A newsletter can condense and coordinate information for everyone involved.

DMSO is increasingly an objective of government action: legislation and regulation. For example, several states already have legalized DMSO within their borders; and several others have bills in hearing or in preparation. Only a newsletter can keep track of such developments and report them in accurate, timely fashion to readers with special interests.

Our policy will be to treat DMSO as one case among many in modern biomedical research. **It is not a special case of the miraculous**. On the other hand, it is clear that its unorthodox characteristics do not fit normal expectations about biomedical substances. The emergence of DMSO is not likely to conform to standard patterns of research and development. There is a special need for informed understanding.

Our Response to the Controversy

The "controversy" surrounding DMSO has both a superficial and a profound dimension. The superficial controversy concerns the way the press handles the story. The deeper aspects reveal inadequacies in the biomedical community and its relation to the general public.

No one in the biomedical community said or did anything clearly inappropriate concerning DMSO. A parallel controversy occurred 15 years later in the handling of the public debate over recombinant DNA. The Asilomar Group that chose to alert the public to the potential dangers of recombinant DNA research was not prepared for the popular interpretation or response.

Early proponents of DMSO probably regret some overly enthusiastic statements, just as the Asilomar Group regrets its early representations. What we have learned is that neither the public nor the scientific community is well prepared to discuss and evaluate all issues related to any biomedical substance or technology. A better form is needed.

The deeper aspect of the DMSO controversy raises questions about the place of science in the greater society. Who should direct research and development in the biomedical community? Who should finance it - the public or commercial ventures? Is the government's peer review system adequate to deal with advances that don't fit into preconceived categories or programs? Is the role of the FDA in regulation well-conceived? Does emphasis on short-term profit among drug companies suppress innovation?

We hope to respond to these problems concerning science and society in two ways. First, by acting as an intermediary in the scientific as well as the social debate about DMSO, we will invite guest editorials and encourage letters to the editor. When exaggerated statements are made one way or the other, we will meet them with qualifications and clarification and a broader base of information. Using a journal, or in this case, a professional newsletter, as a forum is already a well-established tradition in the scientific community.

Our second response, however, is new and different. Through the newsletter we hope to establish more direct links between the researcher, the practitioner and the public at large. More direct communication will bring better understanding. We will follow the example of the Hastings Center Institute of Society, Ethics and the Life Sciences, a leader in fostering calm and reasoned professional standards for communication on biomedical issues with significant social and political dimensions. We will adopt their high standards.

Whenever possible, we will promote a sound and coordinated research policy to advance understanding of the biological actions of DMSO. We plan an active information program to supplement the newsletter as technical support to researchers. Where appropriate, we will help to organize discussions and symposiums to these ends.

1

HISTORY AND LEGAL STATUS

Dr. Stanley Wallace Jacob, Associate Professor of Surgery at the Oregon Health Sciences University, the reputed "father of DMSO" discovered, together with Robert Herschler, a Crown Zellerbach chemist, the therapeutic potential of DMSO.

A Brief History Of DMSO

Eight decades passed from the first recorded synthesis of DMSO to the investigation of its biological usefulness. Like so many other compounds, once synthesized and its simplest properties catalogued, there was no immediate motivation to explore its potential usefulness. It was a time in the history of chemistry when the world was overwhelmed by new immediate industrial opportunities, but underfinanced in research and development activities.

Both technological and economic needs in the early 1950's reawakened both commercial and scientific interest in DMSO. There was a technological need for a superior solvent in the new polymer industries.

An unrelated world-wide research effort was underway to utilize forest-derived waste chemicals such as lignin. The lignin turns out to be one of the many potential sources of the methyl groups needed to prepare DMS. Virtually all DMSO is manufactured from a feed stock of DMS.

Commercial utilization of DMSO was first undertaken in about 1953. The first manufacturing plant was started by Stepan Chemical Company in the United States. In this pioneering effort, DMSO was promoted with emphasis on its superior solvent properties. Another line of development attempted to substitute DMSO for ethylene glycol as an anti-freeze additive to coolant waters.

Lovelock and Bishop showed it was possible to utilize this property of DMSO to protect cells against freezing damage. Their publication in 1959 is the first record of experimentation with DMSO in a biological system.

The research exploring the biological actions of DMSO in organisms in normal conditions began in 1959 with Robert Herschler and Stanley Jacob. They were initially interested in the ability of DMSO to move across membranes, and to carry some dissolved substances with it. These experiments employed both animals and plants. Initially, their investigations included four other solvents: dimethyl formamide (DMF), dimethyl acetamide (DMAC) and acetone. These were later dropped due to toxicities seen in several biological systems.

The important biological effects discovered in the initial inquiries by Herschler and Jacob, that stimulated later clinical evaluations, included:

1. Penetrates membranes and "carries" other substances with it.
2. Decreases inflammation.
3. Relieves pain.
4. Inhibits growth of bacteria.
5. Acts as a diuretic (increases urine volume).
6. Improves effectiveness of antibiotics.
7. Relieves swelling caused by trauma.
8. Relaxes muscles.
9. Improves blood flow.

What Is The Legal Status Of DMSO?

DMSO has been approved for prescriptive use in a 50 percent concentration. Any physician may prescribe it as he/she deems appropriate - but the FDA did not always consider this to be the case.

Amendments to the Food and Drug Act in the early 1960's increased the regulatory jurisdiction of the FDA. Previously they were charged only with overseeing the safety of any preparation sold to the public. Now they were also responsible for making sure that any drug sold to the public was also effective for advertised use. The law was intended to slow down the rate at which new drugs were entering the marketplace, and hopefully, to raise standards. A key part of the story of DMSO is the fact that it was caught between two different standards of formal approval. The additional requirement, to prove effectiveness or "efficacy," meant that a drug must be approved separately for each condition, or ailment, where it was felt it might be beneficial. Up to 1978 the FDA took a position that a physician could not prescribe a drug for an unapproved medical application.

On September 28, 1978 the Courts decided that the FDA had no jurisdiction in trying to "regulate medical practice." Its jurisdiction covered only the advertisement and certain aspects of the sale of a drug. This opened a door for physicians to prescribe DMSO for any condition, where, in their professional judgment, it might be of benefit to a patient.

Unfortunately, most physicians are still unclear about their legal position in this area. The recent increase in malpractice claims has led some to feel that even though perfectly legal, prescription of a drug for an application not approved by the Washington bureaucracy might leave them open to malpractice suits. But there is little reason to believe that approval by a group of bureaucrats would reduce the possibility of a malpractice suit.

Medical practice is overseen by State Boards of Medical Examiners and non-governmental Associations of Physicians. Furthermore, the scientific evidence is what carries weight, not the interpretation of that evidence by a few government appointed professionals, who are often closely tied to the pharmaceutical industry. In addition, the potential scope of judgments by the government medical officers is highly restricted by the requirements of regulatory statutes - passed by legislators, not physicians.

Physicians' Right to Prepare and Dispense

Each physician has the traditional right to prepare and dispense drugs to his own patients. One easily forgets that the domination of the multi-national pharmaceutical firms and the FDA is relatively recent in history. Many physicians regularly prescribe RIMSO-50, the 50% DMSO preparation available through Research Industries Corporation of Utah. Others, aware of their legal position, have moved to purchase highly purified DMSO from the

Physicians and pharmacists have been largely unaware or confused about their right to prepare and dispense DMSO. This unfortunate circumstance has arisen because of the FDA's aggressive interpretation of their new powers under the 1960 Amendments to the Food and Drug Act. In 1978 the Courts strongly reaffirmed the physicians rights and responsibilities as fully independent of FDA jurisdiction.

chemical industry or veterinary suppliers, then converting it into a pharmaceutical for their own use on particular patients. By using the veterinary and highly purified industrial grades, the physician is able to prepare DMSO in the more generally useful clinical concentrations, 70% - 90%.

Several states have passed legislation specifically giving approval to physicians to prescribe DMSO for conditions other than interstitial cystitis (The FDA approved application (1978) for RIMSO-50 is for interstitial cystitis. This is a relatively rare, painful inflammation and scarring of the bladder.) These new statutes serve to reaffirm what is already established by case precedent. This process of reaffirming through statute, often clarifying the situation, is a common practice in the law.

One Legal Maneuver

Once one understands the legal situation, it becomes clear why Research Industries Corporation decided in 1974-1975 to concentrate its efforts to secure approval of DMSO for interstitial cystitis and scleroderma. These are not common conditions. Total number of persons suffering from both conditions in the U.S. is under 150,000. This is by no means enough potential users to recover the costs of research, development and the expensive compliance procedures.

R.I. hoped that physicians would prescribe DMSO in the really important major clinical areas - sports injuries and inflammatory diseases (like arthritis) - once it became available in general. By and large, this has not occurred, although it is gradually taking off. Physicians are more conservative (or less informed) than the R.I. strategy assumed. While on the subject, many proponents of DMSO believe that the only reason approval for scleroderma was denied (or perhaps the appropriate term is "delayed"), is because it would have made a 70% DMSO solution easily available to the physician in a pharmaceutical grade. The 50% DMSO concentration used in interstitial cystitis is expected to be less effective in the major clinical applications.

Legislative Strategies

Two new legislative strategies have recently emerged in the States of Washington and Oregon. In April of 1981, the Washington Legislature passed a bill, later signed by Governor Spellman, to make DMSO an over-the-counter drug. The new law directs the State Board of Pharmacy to regulate the manufacture, labeling, distribution and sale. The main difficulty with the bill is that it requires the DMSO to be manufactured within the state. At the moment there is only one manufacturing plant for DMSO in the United

States, located in Bogaloosa, Louisiana. It is unlikely that anyone will start a plant in Washington just to comply with this new law. In any case, the law may well be superfluous. As long as DMSO is totally manufactured, labeled and sold within a state, the FDA lacks jurisdiction - derived normally from the "interstate commerce" clause of the U.S. Constitution. The Washington law does indicate the political climate. It passed almost unanimously. And the situation has been the same in other states. The people want action on this issue.

Oregon was the first to initiate laws, in 1978, to permit DMSO to be prescribed by physicians within the state for ailments other than interstitial cystitis. The law reaffirms the legal rights of the physician. In June 1981, Oregon initiated a new legislative strategy. The legislature passed a bill asking Congress - via the Oregon delegation - to direct the FDA to exempt Oregon from DMSO regulation.

The key part of the request is to allow DMSO, brought into the state across interstate boundaries, to be exempted from FDA regulation. Governor Atiyeh wrote individual letters to each member of the Oregon delegation requesting that they work together to introduce federal legislation to accomplish this. The second part of the bill sets up a regulatory system within the State of Oregon to ensure the quality and proper labeling of DMSO sold within the state. A special fund is to be created from a $1 levy on each bottle of DMSO sold. This fund would finance research on DMSO and facilitate the dissemination of accurate information about DMSO to the public. This second part of the bill takes effect if, and only if, the Federal Congress passes the exemption.

This is the only legislative strategy so far that is likely to have a real impact on availability of pharmacist-approved medical grade DMSO - in fact, much of what is already available on the people's medical market is medical grade DMSO, but much of it isn't. And for the consumer, it is impossible to tell the difference.

The International Legal Status

Internationally, DMSO has been a general prescriptive agent in the Soviet Union since 1971, and is widely used. The Russians and East Germans are perhaps slightly ahead of the rest of the world in DMSO research. It is only every few years that occasional articles reviewing their knowledge are translated into English. The last book and major review article were translated in 1975. In West Germany and Austria, it is prescriptive in the treatment of acute and chronic musculoskeletal disorders (sports-like injuries and arthritis). Spain made DMSO prescriptive some years ago, and one report rates it as the single most widely used preparation. DMSO has been prescriptive in several other European countries at one time or another. In many cases, physicians make DMSO preparations for their particular

patients. DMSO is available in Canada for scleroderma on a prescriptive basis. In most of South America DMSO is prescriptive for arthritis, bursitis, burns, sprains and strains.

What Went Wrong?

To understand what has happened, one must first recognize that there are three or four possible processes that can lead to a drug receiving FDA approval, to be advertised and sold under label for a particular ailment.

In all cases a drug must be promoted by one or another institution or exceptional individual in the society. The FDA is a passive regulatory bureaucracy; it does not undertake research and development to bring new drugs or therapies to the public.

By far the most important promoters during this century have been the commercial pharmaceutical houses. Tied for second and third are the National Institutes of Health (NIH) and the research arms of the various Medical Schools. A poor fourth is the dedicated individual researcher. There are reasons why each of the leading three failed with DMSO.

The Failures of the Pharmaceutical Firms

The pharmaceutical firms did launch major research and development efforts in the early 1960's. Merck, Squibb and Schering A.G., and Syntex, all undertook multi-million dollar programs to bring DMSO to the market place. Their studies concentrated on sports-type injuries and arthritis. Figured in 1980 dollars, the three multi-nationals spent something like two hundred million dollars, and evaluated close to one hundred thousand patients. Only summaries on about six thousand of these cases have ever been reported in the scientific literature. To this day, these companies maintain a top secret classification on this data. Why? Because they paid for it and research data is an expensive product, not to be given away for nothing.

Later, in 1965, the FDA terminated human clinical studies with DMSO. This decision was made on the basis of toxicity findings in a Merck-supported study in lower animals. The toxicity was noted in terms of changes in the lens of the eye. At the time, no other researchers, public or private, had witnessed a single case of serious toxicity in man. Clinical termination of the drug, therefore, came as a great surprise and a grave disappointment to many physicians familiar with DMSO. A series of reviews, as well as major new toxicity studies, established that the lens change does not occur in humans or monkeys, only in lower animals. These later studies served to establish DMSO as one of the safest research drugs in medical history.

The Failure of the Relation to the FDA

Three applications to market DMSO were submitted in 1965 prior to the toxicity scare. These were turned down for complex reasons. In part the argument was that the studies were not adequately double-blinded. DMSO has an odor so the patient knew when he was receiving the drug - and his desire to please the physician might be the real reason behind any improvements.

The FDA was also much stricter in the 1960's because of the thalidomide incident. The FDA had withheld its approval for thalidomide when other countries had accepted the limited data on its safety. Outside the U.S. the result was several hundred deformed children (thalidomide was given as a sort of tranquilizer during pregnancy).

Another factor working against approval was that many professionals were concerned with the large number of new drugs being admitted to the market, many with serious potential side effects. Legislation was passed to slow things down and raise standards.

Congress had amended the Food and Drug Act to require pharmaceutical firms, not only to prove safety - the earlier emphasis - but also now to prove that the drug actually works. This latter requirement had previously been a matter for each individual physician to decide. What is more, the new law required that the drug not only work for the ailment for which it was advertised, but must be shown to **work better** than any currently available medication or treatment. This immediately lead to a doubling and quadrupling of the cost to bring a drug to market. And the FDA all of a sudden took on the new role of regulator of medical practice. What could and could not be prescribed for a particular illness or condition now had to be approved by the FDA - at least according to the FDA.

The Overall Commercial Problem

The above factors are the ones normally cited by the insiders as to (1) why the FDA rejected the early applications to market DMSO, and (2) why the pharmeutical companies decided not to pursue DMSO any further.

One other major consideration entered into the mid-1960's: cost/benefit analysis. Pharmaceutical companies had to decide whether it was worth their while to pursue DMSO research despite the initial temporary setback. Almost no one believed, even then, that there was a serious toxicity problem with DMSO. The question was whether it would be worth the money to prove that there wasn't. The FDA officials in charge were deliberately antagonistic to DMSO and made this known to the pharmaceutical companies. It has been suggested that some officials wanted to make their career by "burying DMSO once and for all." This sort of resistance is not insurmountable but to battle it with some reasonable expectation of success is an expensive process.

In the last few years, however, particularly since the 1978 court decision, this situation has changed. The FDA has been largely cooperative and encouraging to both private and public research institutions.

Another major consideration in cost/benefit analysis still stands and will remain the major obstacle. Once the pharmaceutical firms took a careful look at whether they could eventually expect to profit from DMSO, they realized it was, at best, unlikely.

The reasons in brief were that:

(1) DMSO was patented by the University of Oregon Health Sciences Center, and Crown Zellerbach, who had licensed it widely so no one company could have a relative monopoly to help recover its initial investment. (This reflects the failure of our national policy on patents and is not the fault of any of the participants in DMSO research and development.)

(2) DMSO competes directly with a wide range of already established drugs and therapies that currently represent the profitbase of the major pharmaceutical companies;

(3) even if a company were to switch emphasis to DMSO, it could not keep the price high enough to recover its initial costs.

This problem is quite real as evidenced by the "DMSO-as-solvent" People's Market (black market). One way or another, the People's Market will always undersell the pharmaceutical companies. It must be emphasized as before that this situation is no one's fault. The president or board of directors of pharmaceutical firms only have a certain amount of assets to work with. If they spend their money on products for which they can never recover their investment, they will soon go bankrupt.

The Medical Center Option

It is at this point that many people feel the NIH (National Institutes of Health) and tax-supported research activities of the nation's medical schools should have entered the picture. What happened at NIH was largely an extension of the antagonistic stance of the FDA. Research proposals to explore the biological actions of DMSO were rejected as "drug-testing" - not appropriate as pure research.

To be fair, there has been a wide-ranging policy problem of whether the government should help support research on medications or technologies that have been patented, either by private or public bodies. Many advances could be cited. Support was denied once commercial development began, in particular, once a patent had been applied for. On the other hand, numerous other projects - such as computers and current biotechnology research - have been massively supported by government research grants. This government funding occurred not only despite commercial developments, but clearly and deliberately to help and encourage movement of these products to the market place.

It would have been appropriate for NIH to support DMSO research and development in the 1960's, and particularly in the 1970's (when the dilemma for the pharmaceuticals was clear). But they didn't. Whether their failure to support should be attributed to bureaucratic incompetence or to a lack of courage is an open question. This is the failure of the second pathway to DMSO approval.

A lack of courage seems to be the principal explanation for the minimal research on DMSO undertaken by the major medical centers. All these centers have private funds of their own. Any one of them could have put together an impressive and decisive research effort on DMSO over a period of five to ten years. Not one medical research center adopted such a policy.

Even the University of Oregon Health Sciences Center, where DMSO research received its initial impetus, has remained largely passive, and occasionally antaganostic to DMSO.

Oregon Health Sciences University, Portland, Oregon (previously University of Oregon Health Sciences Center). Here is where the original research on DMSO was undertaken. OHSU (or The State of Oregon) holds the patents on medical applications of DMSO, together with Crown Zellerbach Corporation.

The Role of the Scientific Community

To appreciate the failure of the nation's medical centers to follow-up on DMSO, one must understand the puritanical attitudes of the scientific community, and how inordinately important is the reputation of the researcher and the institution. Without a progressive, wholesome reputation, you don't receive any money.

Bureaucracies are naturally conservative, whether private or public. Taking on a controversial project is risky and unattractive.

What repelled the vast majority of potential researchers and their institutions was what happened to DMSO in the popular press. The treatment of DMSO as a miracle drug and as a panacea offended the scientific community.

Again, it is really difficult to place the blame - Was it the irresponsible press coverage? Was it premature release of the positive results? Most solid data from the early period has yet to be reported. Or was it the conservative snobbery of the scientific community?

There is something to be said for each of the first two possibilities, but the last hypothesis clearly dominates. Those individual researchers who persisted can testify to the childish harassment - the snickers and rude comments - experienced at scientific meetings and from generally uninformed colleagues.

The following remarks are from an interview with Dr. Jack de la Torre, one of the most courageous and innovative pioneers of DMSO research:

> "Soon (early 1960's) there were hundreds of publications reporting on 'miraculous cures' with the drug, for everything from ingrown toenails to vascular headaches. There is still some stigma attached to the drug due to the overenthusiasm of this period.
>
> "We always played down the effects of DMSO because the drug had had a 'miraculous' label attached to it. Scientists tended to elbow each other at meetings and giggle, implying, 'how can anything be that good?'
>
> "I think when more scientists learn to accept this not as a miracle drug, but as a drug with many potential uses, perhaps they will be stimulated to go to their laboratories and begin to do some of this work. In the meantime, I do not see many people giggling anymore; they are beginning to suspect that there is something to this after all." (**Reports**, Spring 1977; Pritzker School of Medicine, University of Chicago.)

This is the nature of the failure of the third potential pathway to DMSO acceptance.

The Courage of the Individual Researcher

Having made these criticisms of the members of the scientific community and their institutions, one must point out that nonetheless 3500 research papers pertinent to the medical uses of DMSO have been published since 1959. These are attributable to those courageous individuals who were able to see the real potential, beyond the public image of DMSO. These scientists literally put their careers on the line. In many cases, they worked to raise the very funds required, and in more than one instance, the money came from their own pockets to carry on their research.

Their stories will one day make a volume that will be a valuable contribution to understanding the sociology of the scientific community. DMSO research has advanced primarily as a result of the efforts of the individualistic free-enterprise scientist. These exemplary citizens have kept DMSO alive when our normal institutions, our normal mechanisms of normal research and development for pharmaceutical products, have failed.

This fourth pathway is what has kept DMSO alive and has made possible its limited FDA approval. Gradually, as the evidence produced through this pathway mounts, commercial interest is being rekindled.

How To Obtain DMSO

There are basically three ways for the consumer to obtain DMSO at the moment. First, it may be prescribed by your physician as a pharmaceutical product. Second, you may be able to convince a veterinarian to sell you some to treat your pet. Third, there are numerous "solvent distributors" making up the "people's market."

Acquiring DMSO from your physician should be simple and straightforward. However, physicians are still largely uninformed about their rights in this area, and cautious about what they see as moving outside normal channels. Some physicians ask their patients to sign an "informed consent" form, and you might suggest this to your physician if he is not otherwise prepared to accept responsibility.

Medical Grade Through Your Physician

There are two other problems in obtaining DMSO through your physician. The prescriptive, pharmaceutical grade DMSO is only available in a 50% concentration (in 50% water). And the cost of this product, RIMSO-50, available from only one manufacturer (Research Industries) through your pharmacist is currently $14 for a small two ounce vial.

For most applications, the 50% concentration is too weak. The penetration of the skin takes almost twice as long, and many of the effects are significantly reduced or more difficult to obtain. On the other hand, this is clearly the safest DMSO available. Besides being quite pure, the DMSO has been sterilized and monitored for pyrogens. The pyrogen monitoring is a super-precaution.

Is Medical Grade Necessary?

A pyrogen is anything that will cause a detectable fever in a laboratory animal (or person); **pyro-**, means fire, **-gen**, means causes or generates. In reality, pyrogens can be any of a wide range of substances, for instance, a small particle of some toxin floating in the air that has, by chance, found its way into a batch of DMSO.

Most medical professionals informed on the question agree that pyrogen testing is unnecessary for DMSO designed to be applied topically. RIMSO-50 is designed for use in the treatment of interstitial cystitis - where the DMSO is administered through the urethra into the bladder. Whether pyrogen testing is necessary here is an issue still debated by medical professionals.

Pyrogen testing is extremely expensive - one must house and monitor a large number of rabbits and take their temperatures regularly. It has been charged by some DMSO insiders that the fact that the FDA required this extreme precaution of debatable value is an example of their bureaucratic inadequacy. They have been charged by Congress to aid in bringing drugs to the market that are both safe **and** low-cost. (Pyrogen testing has nothing to do with efficacy.) By requiring processing for unnecessary added safety, they have violated the second - low cost - part of their charter. Or so at least it has been charged.

The need for sterilization is also questionable, since at these concentrations, DMSO is self-sterilizing. DMSO is bacteriostatic - it stops (-static) the growth of bacteria at and above 35% DMSO concentration. The sterilization process merely involves filtering the DMSO through a fine "millipore filter." This serves to remove any bacteria-sized particles. This does not add a great deal to the cost of the pharmaceutical grade product.

The advantage of obtaining the pharmaceutical grade DMSO is that its entire processing is more closely monitored than any of the others. There is almost no danger of receiving a contaminated product. And a hopeful note: RIMSO-70, a 70% DMSO solution in water may become available, prescriptively, within the next two or three years.

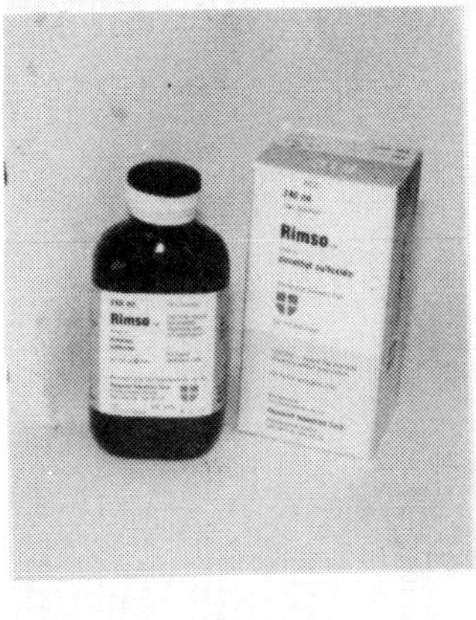

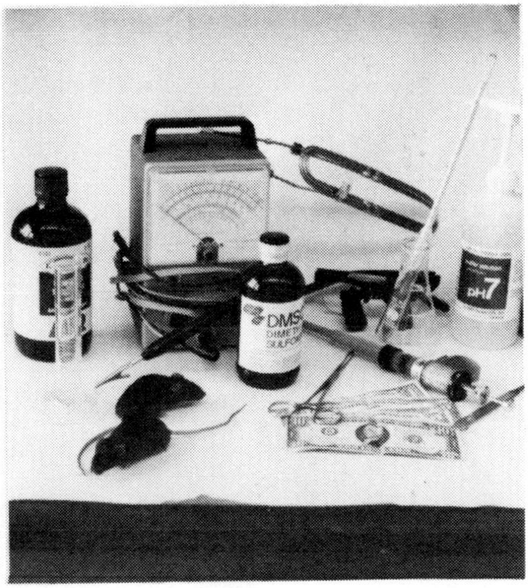

A major source of DMSO for many people in the past has been their local veterinarian. DMSO has proved useful for a wide range of major and minor veterinary problems. Apparently, this avenue to obtain DMSO is most common among horse owners. And no one keeps track of exactly where the DMSO goes. Dog and cat owners have found this more difficult, since muscle injuries, for instance, are not a common dog or cat problem.

Veterinarians have normally insisted on making sure you have a legitimate animal use. But this just leads to counterstrategy. There is one story about a little arthritic poodle making the rounds of most of the veterinary clinics in a major metropolitan area.

Veterinary DMSO is available in 70%, 90%, and 100% (99.5%) concentrations, either as a liquid or gel. The claimed purity is 99.5% - it can, of course, be purer. A reliable source has stated that veterinary grade DMSO and pharmaceutical grade DMSO "come out of the same barrel." This is difficult to confirm because of the secrecy maintained by the firms involved. It may be that the veterinary grade is not as pure, or that it contains a small amount of water - counted as an impurity. It is safe to say that there is no published evidence to show that the veterinary grade DMSO is any less pure than pharmaceutical. The veterinary grade DMSO, however, has not been filter-sterilized and is not pyrogen tested.

The main difficulty with this source of supply is that it places the veterinarian in an uncomfortable - compromising - position. Unlike the DMSO distributed as a solvent, veterinary DMSO is labeled as being a drug. Both the government and the professional associations of veterinarians have tried hard to discourage dispensing DMSO where there is suspicion it is intended for human use.

The veterinarian is very probably liable if anything adverse occurs - that is if he knew or suspected you intended it for human use. Moreover, "looking the other way" is basically unethical and although perhaps not one of the more serious violations of professional conduct, it has been argued that it detracts from the image of the veterinarian as a disciplined professional.

A few veterinarians concerned about their legal position have asked customers to sign statements of intent. The cost of the veterinary DMSO

appears to vary from an extraordinarily low range to the high range in the vicinity of the pharmaceutical RIMSO-50.

The People's Market

The People's Market: This source of supply, sometimes called the black market, is diverse and not directly regulated. The suppliers range from experienced businessmen employing chemists as quality control consultants, to "Cousin Joe" who bottles it in his garage and sells it off the back of his pick-up truck at the local flea market. The only regulation, besides normal market place dynamics, is the Fair Labeling and Packaging Act. This requires that the product be fully labeled, including listing of ingredients, concentration and the name and address of the manufacturer and/or distributor.

Availability of DMSO as a Solvent

DMSO sold as a solvent, or one way or another as a non-pharmaceutical, is commonly found in health-food stores, gas stations, garden and plant shops, hardware and variety stores, and in an increasing number of large grocery stores. Safeway stores spokesmen have stated that they are interested in carrying quality-assured DMSO.

Many outlets are waiting for clarification of their legal position. Your corner drugstore may ultimately be one of the best places. Most drugstores carry a range of non-pharmaceutical products, from cosmetics to lighter fluid, so there is no direct implication that a product sold in such an establishment is being advertised as a pharmaceutical.

The main advantage here is that your local pharmacist is most likely to be highly discriminating and able to exercise professional judgment in his purchasing. If it is true that "98% of the DMSO used for non-industrial purposes in the United States between now and the year 2000 will not be FDA- approved," then the pharmacists have an important role and responsibility in educating and practically managing bottlers and distributors of DMSO in small quantities. Ask your pharmacist for help. Ask him to take responsibility for quality assurance. No one is better qualified in terms of educational background and experience.

If your pharmacist needs more information on DMSO, have him write for the **Pharmacist's Guide to DMSO**, available through the **DMSO News Service**.

What is a Reasonable Cost?

The cost of DMSO obtained through the People's Market has ranged between $5 and $25 for an 8 oz., 1/2 pint bottle at any concentration - 50%, 70%, 90% or 100%. Bottlers figure that although there is less DMSO in preparations of lower concentration, there is more labor involved in preparing mixtures. The average price of $15.95 for a half-pint of 100% DMSO is reasonable, considering the investments, uncertainties and costs of bottling, distribution and retailing.

Since DMSO is not widely available in many areas, the expense of a force of full-time salesmen doubles the cost to the retailer. Several of the large volume People's Market distributors are employing experienced chemical and pharmaceutical salesmen. Your cost with a major distributor may be a little higher, but your chances of obtaining a properly handled and prepared product are much better.

Consider a half-pint bottle of DMSO. The cost of the DMSO to the distributor ranges from 50 cents to a dollar when purchased in bulk. The bottle and label and the bottling and labeling process add approximately two dollars. Administrative overhead (i.e., identifying sources, purchasing, quality assurance, billing, handling, storage, managing a sales force, travel, etc.) add another one dollar. The cost to the wholesaler or salesmen is often in the range of $3.50 to $5. The cost to the retailer, the health-food store, or whatever, ranges correspondingly from a low of $3.50 to a high of $9. The cost to the consumer is between $12 - $18.

Clearly it is possible that some retailers are obtaining bottled and labeled solvent DMSO for $3 and selling it directly to consumers for $18. This is a large mark-up, but it is by no means out-of-line with numerous other products. Cosmetics and vitamins, for instance, frequently have been reported to have mark-ups well in excess of the mark-up for DMSO.

The other thing to keep in mind is that in most cases each person along the "mark-up" route is providing a real and valuable service.

For those unfamiliar with normal product mark-up policies: a television that cost the manufacturer $50 in parts, overhead and labor to make, is sold to a wholesale distributor for $100. The retailer purchases it for $200. He places it in his store and advertises it. The consumer buys it for $400 to $600.

In the future, when the lines of distribution are more stabilized, and the risk to the providers is less, we can anticipate a price of $7.50 to $9.50 for a half-pint of extremely pure, 100% DMSO. Medical grade DMSO that has been sterilized and pyrogen tested will be more expensive.

The Importance of Proper Packaging

DMSO should be contained in either glass, polyethylene or polyurethane bottles. The caps also should be polyethylene or polyurethane. Even in glass bottles they should be "polyseal" caps. These caps have a polyethylene cone

inside to prevent the DMSO from coming into contact with the black-plastic (phenol) cap.

Metal-coated lid liners and fiber lid liners are not acceptable for caps. DMSO will react and form a toxic complex with the metal. And DMSO will dissolve the glue used to bind the fiber.

If you encounter DMSO that has been stored in a container with an unacceptable cap - discard it. Most, if not all, the major distributors have taken the time and effort to inform themselves about proper packaging.

Mixing Your Own

DMSO can be obtained in concentrations ranging from 50% to 100%. Most, if not all, applications call for something less than 100%. The way DMSO is being priced at the moment, you receive the most for your money if you buy 100%. One other advantage of buying 100% is that if there is any contamination from the distributor's processing, it is most likely to have occurred when he mixes the DMSO. If he doesn't have to mix, then he can dispense directly from bulk 55 gallon barrels into small containers.

The main disadvantage of doing your own diluting is that it is also the step where **you** are most likely to contaminate what you have purchased. Another possible problem is that you will forget to dilute your DMSO; see Side Effects.

Three problems face the person who chooses to mix their own: what to mix it with, what to mix it in, and what to store it in later.

The first answer is to mix it with distilled water, easily obtained at a hardware (for steam irons) or grocery store. (NOTE: There has recently been some problems with distilled water in plastic containers. If it smells "plasticky" after it has been poured into a glass - don't use it. The FTC is trying to correct this problem at the moment.) Alternatively, you can use bottled drinking water (preferably not the sparkling type) or tap water. If you are uncertain about the quality of your normal tap water, perhaps you shouldn't be drinking it.

You can mix DMSO and water in a glass (or pyrex) bowl or jar, or in a stainless steel container. Avoid ceramics or anything with paint or a glaze on it. Avoid polyvinylchloride (PVC) plastic containers. You can't make any easy generalizations about DMSO and plastic containers. Some are okay, some aren't.

The question of how to store your "now-greater-than-one-half-pint" of diluted DMSO is important. You want to avoid contamination. The best place for most of it is in the original container - assuming it was acceptable to begin with. Unless you know your plastics, better stick to glass for the rest of it. Between the DMSO and the lid, place a small sheet of aluminum foil. DMSO does not significantly dissolve aluminum foil.

When you mix your DMSO with water, you will notice that the mixture becomes rather warm - even somewhat hot to the touch. This is the result of

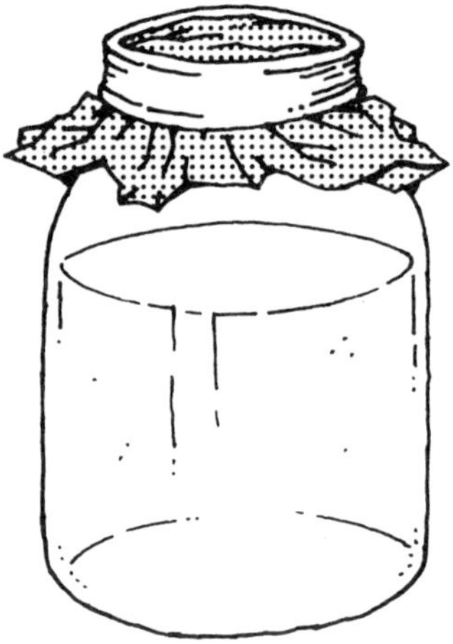

A glass container with either a polyseal lid (polyethylene cone inside the cap) or an aluminum foil liner is the safest way to store excess DMSO after mixing. Otherwise the original container, usually polyethylene, from a major bottler should be safe and reliable for long periods. — Avoid polyvinyl chloride plastic containers. If you don't know what type of plastic a container is made of then **don't use it**.

the dissolution-reaction between DMSO and water. The reaction is to be expected and is perfectly normal. The solution will gradually cool to room temperature.

There is no greater danger with the warm DMSO-plus-water solution if you happen to get some on your skin. Many people have reported a sort of "steam" coming off their hands after contact with DMSO, particularly with high concentrations. You might notice this on a cold morning - it is probably a vapor-phase of DMSO plus water (and perhaps some DMS) much like seeing your breath in cold weather. This occurs as a result of a reaction between DMSO and water in the skin. It will be less noticeable with lower concentrations of DMSO that have already been diluted with water.

Stability, Storage and Shelf-Life (Questions of Purity)

DMSO is a stable chemical product. Stored in glass containers away from excessive heat and/or light, DMSO has demonstrated stability over several years.

It can be heated to 140 degrees C without decomposing. Boiling at 189 degrees C in a self-contained (reflex) system for three days leads to a decomposition of only about 3%. Above this temperature decomposition rapidly accelerates. Heating in the prescence of acid accelerates decomposition.

One hundred percent DMSO is probably slightly more stable than dilutions with water.

A good rule of thumb is to discard any DMSO more than three years old. When in doubt, check the color and odor. Any obvious discoloration or excessive odor is grounds for disposal. If you are still in doubt, discard it. As long as the DMSO has been stored in acceptable containers, there is no serious, increased danger from any of the natural breakdown products except perhaps where there is obvious discoloration or excessive odor.

If human or animal applications are contemplated, store your DMSO as if it were a drug - away from household cleaning agents or garden supplies.

How Can DMSO Be Contaminated?

Although stable by itself, DMSO is easily contaminated by reaction with other substances. It has been found to react with several kinds of plastic containers, cap liners and caps. In general, there are as many possible contaminants as there are substances which will dissolve in DMSO. And DMSO is an excellent solvent for both organic and inorganic substances.

How Can One Detect Contamination?

Identifying any of the myriad possible contaminants requires highly sophisticated equipment that can identify a broad spectrum of chemical compounds. So it is wiser to throw out any suspect DMSO than to engage in enormously expensive testing processes.

Signs that might indicate contamination:

1. Any obviously discolored product.
2. Excessively odorous material.
3. DMSO which has reacted with its container.

(Check the lid - DMSO can dissolve fiber lid inserts and will react with metal-coated lid liners and black plastic (phenolic) caps. It can react with, and literally dissolve, many plastics. Polyethylene and polyurethane, or glass with polyseal caps are safe under normal conditions.)

The best assurance of purity and lack of contamination is to know the history of the DMSO batch. This is where individual state regulations might be helpful. All containers of DMSO must, by law, be labeled with a list of ingredients and the name and address of the manufacturer or bottler-distributor. If you have any problems with DMSO from any source, do not hesitate to contact the company whose name is on the label. Any complaints about mislabeling should be directed to the Consumer Protection Agency of the Department of Commerce.

2

WHAT IS DMSO?

The dimethyl sulfoxide molecule: the particular atoms and their arrangement between properties. Each methyl group is composed of a carbon atom and three hydrogen atoms.

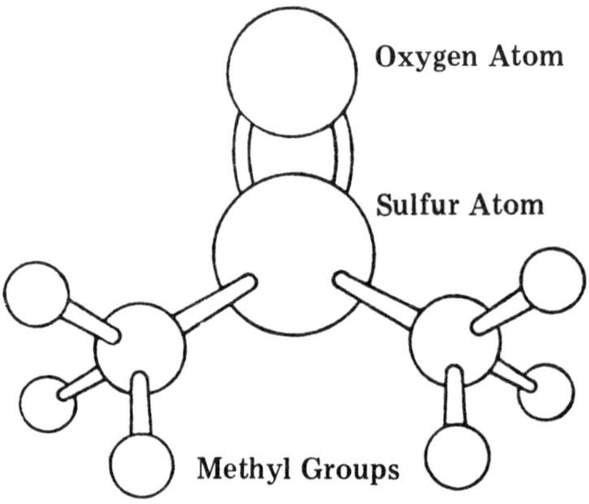

What is DMSO? Physics, Chemistry, Biology

In appearance DMSO is a clear, colorless liquid. It feels slightly oily, tastes bitter, and, surprising to most people, is quite odorless in its pure form. The odor associated with DMSO is really DMS, dimethyl sulfide, a product of the breakdown of DMSO. DMS has a strong garlicky or oyster-like taste and smell.

Physically, DMSO, or dimethyl sulfoxide, is a relatively small molecule. The name describes its atomic structure. Two methyl groups (dimethyl) are attached to one side of a sulfur (sulf-) atom and an oxygen atom (-oxide) to the other side. It is slightly larger than water but much smaller than the giant molecules that make up the structures of living things. The small size is one of the reasons DMSO is able to move easily through the skin and around the body.

Chemically, DMSO is best categorized as a powerful and exceptionally versatile solvent. The best comparisons are with water and alcohol. DMSO is exceptional among solvents because it dissolves inorganic substances (as does water) as well as organic substances (as does alcohol). Furthermore, DMSO will dissolve in water (and vice versa) and in alcohol (and vice versa).

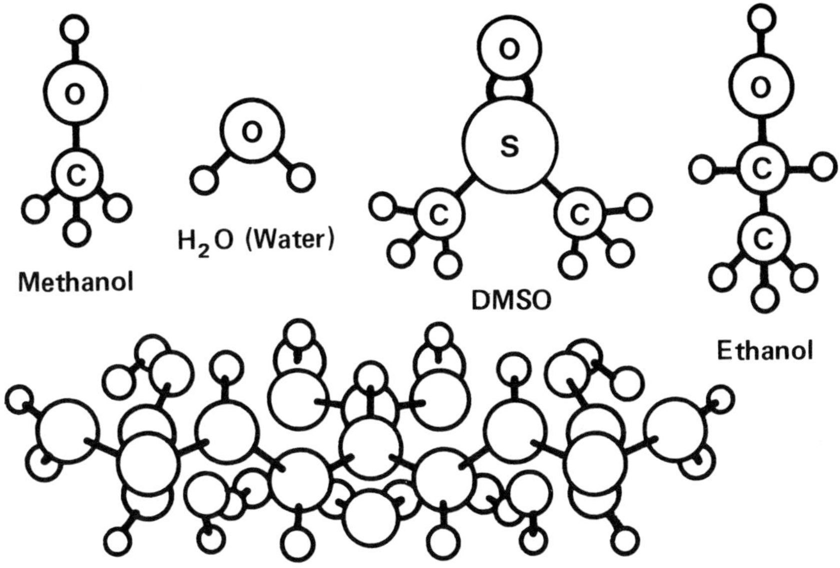

Small portion of a protein molecule

DMSO is a relatively small molecule. It is an excellent solvent, comparable to or better than methyl alcohol (methanol), ethyl alcohol (ethanol; drinking alcohol) and water. In contrast, most of the protein molecules that make up most bodily structures and operators (enzymes) are enormous. As a consequence most solvents, DMSO and water in particular, are able to move around inside the protein molecule structure, sometimes altering the shape and function of the protein.

This dual-solvent characteristic is probably the explanation of DMSO's ability to penetrate the skin. The skin has a dual barrier - one level repels water-based, inorganic substances, the other repels organic substances such as oils and alcohol. DMSO passes through one as an inorganic solvent and then flips-over to pass through the other as an organic solvent.

The chemical interplay of DMSO and water is particularly important. DMSO attracts water very strongly. If you fill a small glass with 100 percent DMSO and leave it overnight on the counter, by morning the glass will be overflowing. The DMSO has attracted water right out of the air. This love-affair with water is the basis of DMSO's anti-freeze property, and many of its biological actions.

Biologically, DMSO and DMS (dimethyl sulfide) are natural substances produced primarily by a variety of soil bacteria during decomposition (or fermentation) of plant material. The freshness of garden vegetables being shipped to market is often determined by measuring the amount of DMS given off by the natural surface bacteria already at work at decomposition. DMS and DMSO are found naturally in beer, resulting from the action of brewer's yeast. Both are regularly present in milk and related products.

Until recently, it was not clear whether bacteria produced DMSO directly or only DMS - while DMSO resulted from a non-biological oxidation. New

studies have shown DMSO is produced by both marine and fresh water algae or plankton, and that bacteria commonly convert DMS to DMSO and back again as needed. Larger sea plants - sea grass in particular - also appear to produce DMSO directly. There is also some preliminary evidence that land plants and trees (oak, cotton, spruce and pine) may produce DMSO during normal growth and metabolism (aside from decay).

How Is DMSO Manufactured?

DMSO is not naturally present in sufficient quantities in plants or trees to make extraction practical. Virtually all DMSO available today is produced by chemical synthesis. The association of DMSO with the wood products industry arose because lignin-cellulose is an excellent source of **methyl groups**. Crown Zellerbach's patented process reacts lignin with molten sulfur to produce DMS. The DMS is then oxidized, resulting in DMSO. An alternative process for initial production of DMS is to react wood alcohol (methanol) with hydrogen sulfide (H_2S). The DMS is then similarly converted by oxidation to DMSO.

More than a million gallons of DMSO a year are manufactured in the United States. All of it comes from a single plant in Bogaloosa, Louisiana, owned by Crown Zellerbach. Small amounts are imported from Aquitaine in France and still smaller amounts from a single Japanese manufacturer.

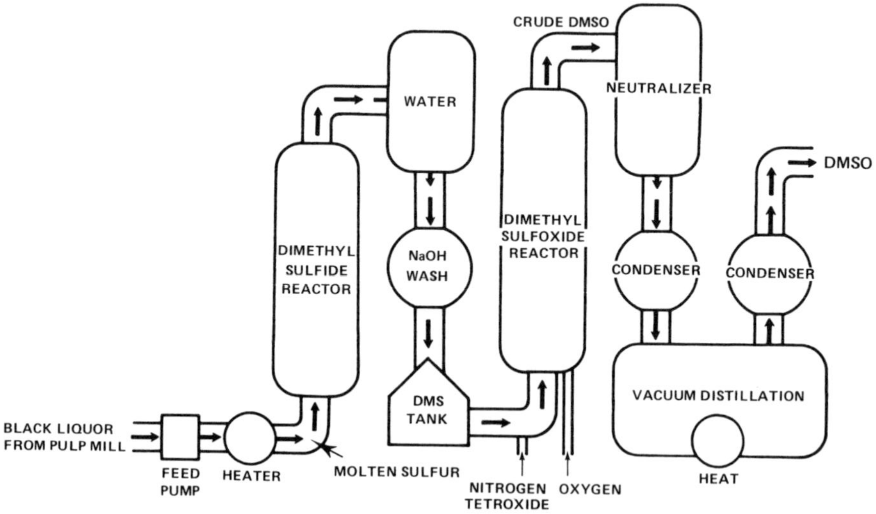

Although there are many ways to synthesize DMSO, virtually all industrial, veterinary and medical grade DMSO in the United States, produced or imported, is made by reacting dimethyl sulfide (DMS) with oxygen and/or nitrogen tetroxide, another source of reactive oxygen atoms. The DMS itself can come from a variety of processes. The most common in the U.S. is by means of reacting molten sulfur with the black liquor (lignin-cellulose) from pulp mills, which is high in methyl groups.

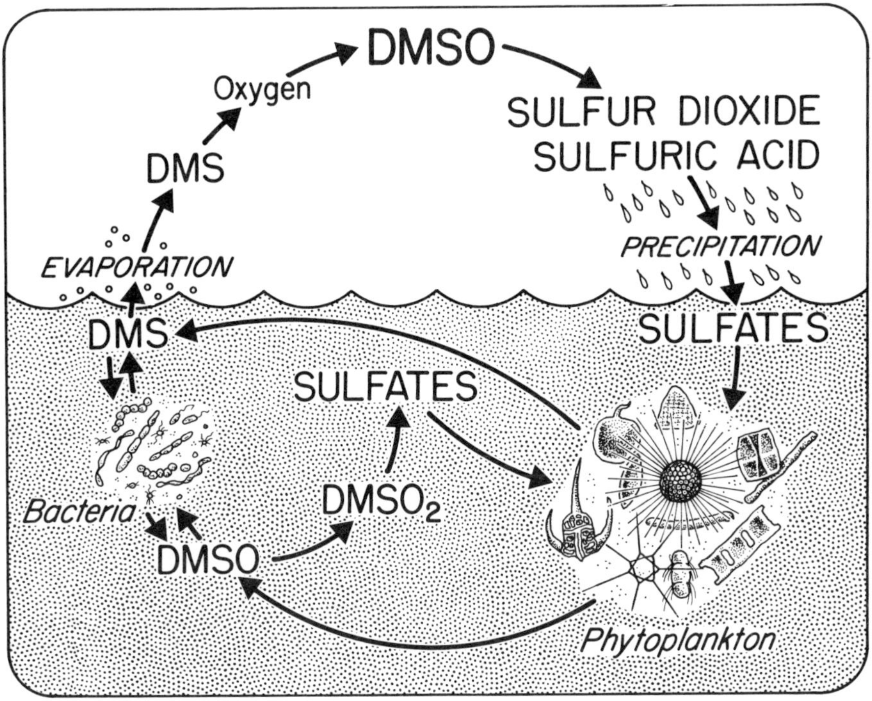

DMS, DMSO, and DMSO2 are all naturally present in the biosphere. DMS is most prevalent, as one of the breakdown products in the normal decay of all plant material. DMSO is present in small amounts in many natural foods and beverages. Recently DMS and DMSO have been found to play a major role in the active (non-decay) metabolism of phytoplankton. This discovery solved a long-standing theoretical problem — concerning the movement of large amounts of sulfur between various regions and realms of the biosphere.

What are the Biological Actions?

The primary biological actions of DMSO, responsible for its recognition as a unique and valuable therapeutic agent, are:

1. Penetration of the skin and transport of dissolved substances.
2. Pain Relief.
3. Anti-inflammatory Action.
4. Improvement of blood flow and reduction of swelling associated with injury.
5. Miscellaneous others needing more research to clarify.

Penetration and transport

DMSO applied topically penetrates several layers of the skin reaching detectable levels in the blood within five minutes. DMSO is not unique in its ability to penetrate the skin. Most substances, particularly small molecules, and most common solvents (water, alcohol, acetone) penetrate the skin and enter the blood. Judged against all substances, however, DMSO's penetration is exceptionally rapid and complete.

The driving force is the mutual attraction of DMSO and water. The importance of the ease of penetration rests in the potential to reach an area of injury or inflammation in a concentrated dose.

DMSO is also able to carry certain other substances through the skin. And this may be of importance in delivering a localized high dose of some medication - particularly to a non-central site, such as an arm or leg.

To help put DMSO's reputation for penetration into perspective, we must recognize that the skin keeps out substances much like clothes keep out dirt. It is far from perfect. Furthermore, there is an old well-known method of delivering substances through the skin that requires nothing more than an occlusive bandage.

Known as the "method of occlusion," it involves merely placing some, more or less airtight bandage or patch over an area of the skin. After it has been in place 24-48 hours, almost any substance placed under the patch will penetrate the skin into the blood stream. We have all experienced the related phenomenon, after removing a bandage that has been in place for some time, and seeing spongy cracks in the skin. Substances placed on such an area pass quickly to the lower layers of the skin and are absorbed (if liquid) into the blood.

This phenomenon is the basis of a new method of delivering medications. If you haven't seen it yet, you will soon. An occlusive patch is placed behind the ear, an area where the skin is particularly thin. The patch itself also contains the medication to be administered. The patch looks rather like a corn-plaster. The medication gradually diffuses out of the patch; this being a new product

development. It penetrates the skin because the presence of the patch has softened and opened passages in the skin.

Notice that there is a new aspirin product being advertised, an aspirin handcream for arthritis. This makes no sense unless the aspirin penetrates through the skin. The product does not contain DMSO. So DMSO is clearly not the only substance which can penetrate the skin.

When spread over the skin, DMSO penetrates - some within seconds, about half within five minutes, and almost all within 15 minutes. From what we know, it is likely that the skin remains fairly open for another half hour, and some precautions are reasonable for up to three hours.

The precaution should be about the same and of the same importance as if you had had an occlusive patch over the area for a day or two. Having penetrated the skin, the DMSO continues to disperse gradually from the site of application throughout the rest of the body. This process is greatly aided, of course, by the circulation of the blood. More than half the dose applied to an area remains in the local tissues after half an hour. But an hour after application, less than 20% remains locally. Gradually, over 24 hours, the DMSO disperses throughout the whole body.

Not all substances can be carried through the skin with DMSO. As a general rule, DMSO will transport only small, non-ionized molecules. Giant molecules of high molecular weight, such as insulin, do not pass through the skin to any significant extent.

An attempt was made to use DMSO in allergy testing by mixing the allergens with DMSO and applying to the skin. However, the subjects only became sensitized to allergens with molecular weights of less than 3000. This strongly suggested that the larger molecules do not pass through easily with DMSO. However, other trials showed that at least some large protein substances will pass through skin treated with DMSO.

Some substances dissolved in DMSO actually pass through the skin much more slowly than the DMSO in which they were dissolved. They must come out of solution as they pass through the skin. Other experiments used various dyes as visual markers of penetration following application of DMSO-dye mixtures to the skin. These showed that there was essentially no penetration of the dye below the first layer of the skin. However, this first layer was completely invaded.

Applications of steroids, including hydrocortisone, with DMSO, showed that the normal penetration of this steroid through the skin into the blood was increased about 3-1/2 times. A reservoir of hydrocortisone can be created in the upper layer of the skin by using DMSO as a carrier substance. This reservoir remains for as long as 16 days, and is resistant to washing with alcohol or soap and water. Some of these experiments led to a major study of the therapeutic potential of a DMSO-hydrocortisone cream in the 1960's by a large pharmaceutical company. The proposed combination was never approved or marketed, although the results were apparently quite positive. (The evidence is the property of the pharmaceutical firm and has still not been made public.)

Our understanding of the mechanism of penetration is still largely incomplete. We do not understand, for instance, why substances are

transported better with 90% DMSO than with 100%. From what we understand, 100% should work better, but it doesn't. Much of the lack of knowledge is not about DMSO particularly, but about the skin itself, its electromechanical properties, the nature of normal repulsions and transport, the submicroscopic detail of the membrane structures. Besides more research on DMSO, we need more basic research to understand the skin as well.

Pain relief

DMSO is an established analgesic (pain reliever). It is effective in a wide range of conditions, from headaches to sports injuries to arthritis. One study treated 37 patients suffering from intractable pain (seen during surgical practice). Pain had been present for over one year in each case. Conventional therapies failed to control it, but 32 of the 37 patients reported remarkable relief after DMSO therapy. The patients included 11 with tic douloureux, 11 with post amputation phantom pain, 10 with post traumatic intractable pain, and 5 with post operative intractable pain.

Henry Haigler and Denise Spring at Emory University School of Medicine in Atlanta Georgia recently reported DMSO was found to produce pain relief in rats that is comparable in magnitude to morphine, although the duration (6-7 hours) is longer than that of comparable amounts of morphine (2 hours). The mechanism of action of DMSO was found to be different from that of morphine as demonstrated by the fact that naloxone, a specific narcotic antagonist (blocking the narcotic effect) does not block the effect of DMSO. No drug dependence occurs with DMSO. It is neither a narcotic nor a barbiturate.

In trials of DMSO for musculoskeletal problems (strains, sprains, acute bursitis and tendonitis), pain was relieved within one hour after treatment with 80% DMSO.

The pain relief obtained with DMSO has been shown to be comparable to what occurs with narcotic pain relievers. However, no cases of drug dependence have been reported with DMSO. A 1981 study showed that naloxone, a substance that blocks the effect of narcotic pain relievers, did not in any way reduce the effect of DMSO. This clearly establishes that the mechanisms of action of DMSO and narcotic pain relievers is fundamentally different.

DMSO is an analgesic (pain reliever), but not an anesthetic (remover of sensation). Unlike narcotics, DMSO still lets you feel what's happening in an area where it has been applied. Pain is reduced but does not completely disappear. This is extremely important in sports medicine where the danger of accidental reinjury due to lack of sensation-awareness is a concern. (See Questions Section for more detail.)

Laboratory experiments have shown that under various circumstances, DMSO can reduce the speed of nerve signal transmission in large nerves. It can completely inhibit transmission in the minor peripheral nerves. Activity returns to normal when DMSO is washed away.

Anti-inflammatory

DMSO has been shown to be effective in reducing inflammation in a wide range of experimental and clinical situations. This has been broadly tested in both animals and humans.

Using a variety of toxins and physical insults, one can create experimental versions of arthritis (local and general), dermatitis, allergic eczema, and inflammations due to several types of tissue damage. DMSO works to decrease the severity of the inflammations in virtually all cases. However, the experiments do show inconsistencies indicating that the manner of application and dosage may be crucial. With one toxin, if DMSO was applied before the toxin, it prevented inflammation; however, if the toxin was applied first, DMSO increased the already present inflammation. Presumably, DMSO acted to spread the toxin, and the action of the toxin was faster than the action of the DMSO to prevent this.

An important early study examined the anti-inflammatory effects of DMSO as compared to, and in combination with, cortisone. Cortisone stabilizes cellular structures, particularly lysosomes, against a variety of injurious agents. Lysosomes are the tiny sacs of powerful digestive enzymes in cells. When inflammation occurs, lysosomes tend to break open, spilling their powerful contents into the cell, killing it, and then the cell spills its toxic contents into the cellular environment. This destroys other cells, releasing more lysosomes, and so forth. The result is a growing, accele- rating, vicious cycle of inflammation and destruction. When coritsone was dissolved in DMSO, the concentration of cortisone necessary to stabilize the lysosome was reduced from 10 to 1000 times. It was suggested that DMSO might provide a

vehicle that makes cortisone more readily available to target tissues, resulting in reduced inflammation.

DMSO has been shown to protect cells from a wide range of stressful stimuli - including heat, cold, ultrasonic vibration and radiation.

An important observation is that in most instances, the anti-inflammatory effects of DMSO usually occur whether the dose is applied topically to the local site, or taken orally, intravenously, or injected at another site. This tells us the DMSO is acting **systemically** on the chemistry of the whole body, not just on conditions at the local site.

Improves blood supply and reduces swelling

DMSO has a definite, and sometimes dramatic, effect in promoting blood flow throughout the body.

The fact that DMSO increases the effects of several other drugs is now believed to be a consequence of this improvement of circulation. The drugs reach their desired targets more effectively.

For a number of years, we knew that DMSO stimulated medium sized blood vessels to enlarge or dilate. And we also knew that DMSO had a dramatic effect in reducing swelling, but these were not seen to be connected. Dilation (opening wider) of the vessels alone would not account for reduction of swelling. In fact, one could argue that it might increase swelling in the extremities. Cold-packs are traditionally applied to reduce swelling because they constrict blood vessels, decreasing the amount of blood entering the area.

During this early period, the dramatic reduction of swelling was hypothesized to be due to DMSO somehow drawing the water out of the swollen tissues.

More recent studies have revealed a cooperative network of effects:

A. Dilation of the large and medium sized blood vessels.

B. Contraction of the tiny capillary vessels.

C. Lessening of adhesion (stickiness) of blood cells and damaged cellular debris.

A black eye, or other major bruise, can often take several weeks to clear. With applications of DMSO, the process takes only a few days. Improved circulation brings nutrients to the surviving cells and helps them to stabilize and repair sooner. Debris is released from the local site and is consumed naturally by special roving white blood cells (called phagocytes).

Experiments on animals have shown that applications of DMSO can increase the chances of successful tissue grafts. This is attributed to the improvement of circulation. In frostbite, the stimulation of circulation is believed to be at least part of the beneficial effect of DMSO.

When disease or injury swells tissues inside the skull, abnormal pressure may do more damage than the original trauma. This pressure is often what causes paralysis and death. DMSO controls elevated pressure inside the skull, bringing it back to normal, typically within five-ten minutes. It was the speed of this effect that finally convinced researchers that the reduction in swelling

could not have been due to a process where DMSO was "pulling water out of the tissues." Only a contraction of the capillary system could explain the rapid decrease in the volume of fluid in the head.

Parallel studies of DMSO therapy in stroke indicate a stimulation of collateral circulation - the back-up system of vessels that can supply an area of tissue. This means that although circulation to the stroke area is blocked by the blood clot (embolism), still the region receives adequate oxygen and nutrients to prevent tissue death. The action of DMSO (via prostaglandins) to reduce adhesion and retard clotting appears also to prevent growth of the embolism - otherwise a frequent problem in stroke.

Other effects needing more research

A number of other actions of DMSO have been reported in the scientific literature. Some are perhaps destined to be more significant than others in clinical application. No one is certain at the moment.

Bacteriostasis. At concentrations of 30%-50%, DMSO strongly inhibits the growth of a wide range of bacteria and fungi, including at least one parasite.

An unusual observation is that several antibiotic-resistant organisms become sensitive to treatment after pre-treatment with DMSO. Several anti-fungal agents are more potent when mixed with DMSO.

There are clearly a number of bacteria that are **not** inhibited by DMSO and do **not** become less resistant to antibiotics. DMSO is **not** a highly effective, universal antiseptic.

There is still some concern that if an already infected area, containing a DMSO-resistant bacteria or viral strain, were treated with DMSO topically,

BACTERIOSTATIC AND BACTERICIDAL EFFECTS OF DMSO ON A GROUP OF SELECTED MICROORGANISMS

Test microorganism	Concentration DMSO used, %a									
	0	1	4	5	10	20	30	40	50	60
Escherichia coli	3	3	3	3	3	1	0	0	0	0
Aerobacter cloacae	3	3	3	3	3	1	0	0	0	0
Pseudomonas aeruginosa	3	3	3	3	2	0	0	0	0	0
Proteus vulgaris	3	3	3	3	3	1	0	0	0	0
Staphylococcus aureus	3	3	3	3	3	2	1	0	0	0
Streptococcus pyogenes	3	3	3	3	3	1	0	0	0	0
Streptococcus faecalis	3	3	3	3	3	2	1	1	0	0
Salmonella schottmulleri	3	3	3	3	2	1	0	0	0	0
Diplococcus pneumoniae	3	3	2	0	0	0	0	0	0	0
Candida albicans	3	3	3	3	1	1	0	0	0	0

*a*O, No growth; 1, light growth; 2, moderate growth; 3, normal or unrestricted growth.
G. E. Pottz, J. H. Rampey, and F. Benjamin (141:214)

spread of the infective agent could produce an extension of the infection. A related concern is that treatment of an infected area could promote the rapid transport of toxins produced by the micro-organism out of the local site. There is no hard evidence of danger. It has even been suggested that transport of toxins out of the infected area might well improve the conditions in favor of healing.

Immune Response. When experimental animals were treated eight days prior to infection, their resistance to the infecting organism was enhanced. In another study, allergy specialists found that by mixing DMSO with low-molecular weight allergens (substances that evoke an allergic response), it is possible to increase sensitization. Neither of these phenomenon is understood, although it is believed that the latter is probably related to the ability of DMSO to transport and help circulate allergens.

More sophisticated studies indicate that DMSO may turn out to be of value in treating a variety of immune deficiency diseases, as well as the auto-immune diseases (myasthenia gravis, lupus, scleroderma, rheumatoid arthritis and so forth).

In auto-immune disease, the immune system mistakenly begins to reject and attack some part of one's own body. One measure of the severity of the problem is the number of auto-immune antibodies present in the person's blood serum. A 1980 animal study at Johns Hopkins University demonstrated that relatively small amounts of DMSO administered over 1-2 weeks could dramatically lower the level of auto-immune antibodies in an experimental version of myasthemia gravis (MG). The reduction was observed to last at least four weeks after cessation of DMSO therapy. Whether DMSO will prove of benefit in human patients with MG is not known. Human trials are expected to begin by early 1982 (if not sooner).

Effect on Collagen. DMSO appears to have a positive effect in collagen (or connective tissue) diseases, and on abnormal deposits of collagen. It does not alter normal collagen or connective tissue. This has been demonstrated in both laboratory chemical experiments and by clinical measurements. In some very provocative animal experiments researchers in both the U.S. and Israel have shown that DMSO prevents the formation of artherosclerosis (hardening of the arteries) in rabbits fed on a high cholesterol diet. This is consistent with the general finding that DMSO alters abnormal collagen processes. Studies are underway to determine whether DMSO might be of some value as therapy after the artherosclerotic plaques have already formed.

Cholinesterase Inhibition. Part of signal transmission between nerves involves the release of special neurotransmitter substances at the intersections between the nerves. After being released, these substances are normally broken down into constituent parts fairly quickly. Cholinesterase is a substance that breaks down one of the common neurotransmitters. A variety of drugs and chemical agents are known to slightly inhibit or slightly enhance the action of cholinesterase. DMSO slightly inhibits cholinesterase.

The effects are general and constitute a stimulation of the parasympathetic nervous system. Specific consequences are a slight tranquilizing effect, relaxation of skeletal muscles, and increased tone of smooth muscle (internal organs). The relaxation of skeletal muscle may be

the basis of other reports of the ability of DMSO to alleviate muscle spasm.

There is also a lowering of the threshold of stimulation of the vagus nerve. The vagus nerve exits the spinal cord at the neck and activates many internal organs as it descends through the central body. The lowering of the threshold of stimulation of the vagus nerve has one rather interesting consequence. Some males have reported spontaneous erections and mild prolongation of erection during sexual activity.

Diuresis. DMSO produces a marked diuretic effect. This means that it increases urine output. With relatively large clinical doses, a series of rats receiving 90% DMSO had a 10-fold increase in urine volume for a brief period. A group of human patients receiving intravenous DMSO on an experimental program were reported to have an increased urine volume and increased excretion of sodium and potassium. This is consistent with the understanding that DMSO operates as a normal osmotic diuretic.

Persons already taking an osmotic diuretic, for instance, to control high blood pressure, should consult their physician before undertaking any long-term DMSO treatments. DMSO does not seem to have any overall effect on the blood pressure, and so is not a substitute for any blood pressure medication.

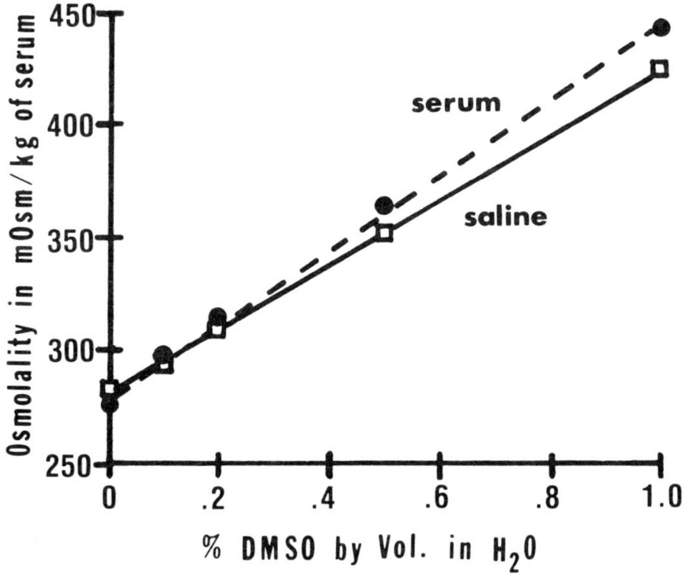

*DMSO increases blood osmolality — drawing water from the tissue spaces into the blood stream. However, since DMSO is bound to plasma proteins in the blood, it is unclear how it accomplishes this effect. The graph shows — enigmatically — that the osmolality increases in the same way whether DMSO is added to serum (with plasma proteins present) or to plain saline (salt solution). One researcher remarked, "Apparently, for each molecular equivalent of dimethyl sulfoxide, bound to protein or other binding substances in the blood plasma, slightly more than one molecular equivalent of osmotically active solute is released." (**Clinical Chemistry**, 26:1745)*

How Does It Work?

It is unlikely that the biological actions of DMSO will ever be explained in terms of one particular property. DMSO, as a bio-substance, has **several** important features. What has been learned over the past 18 years - including results reported in over 3500 published research articles - can be summarized into four main categories.

1. The Relation To Water

The relation of DMSO to water has been suggested as the basis of the most general explanation of the most biological actions of DMSO. DMSO and water are very comfortable together. One may think of it as a sort of love-affair.

When pure DMSO is mixed with water there is a mild binding reaction - the mixture heats up. The reaction does not change the DMSO or the water. Rather one or several types of "chemical complex" are formed. We may conclude that these DMSO + water complexes are more stable than the separate substances swimming around in solution independent of one another. The heat given off by the reaction tells us that in order to separate DMSO + water, a great deal of heat would need to be applied. This is another way of saying the complexes are stable under normal circumstances.

The affair between DMSO and water may be seen in other ways. DMSO is often described as a strong attractor of water. DMSO can pull water right out of the air. Try placing two or three drops of DMSO on one side of a plate and two or three drops of water on the other. Leave this over night. In the morning you will find that the DMSO has increased its size whereas the water has evaporated.

Just as water tends to find its way to DMSO, so too DMSO moves preferentially towards water. Regardless of how or where DMSO is applied to the body, it migrates more to regions with more water. After a couple of hours the amount in the blood, for instance, may be several times greater than the whole body average; the amount in bones and cartilage being several times less than the whole body average. This is simply because the amount of water in the blood is greater than the whole body average, and the amount of water in bones and cartilege is less than the whole body average. A great deal about the movement of DMSO in the body can, therefore, be explained in terms of this strong mutual attraction of DMSO and water.

The formation of the stable DMSO + water complexes helps to explain the action of DMSO as a freeze preservative. DMSO and water bind so tightly that as the temperature is lowered the normal formation of water crystals - ice - is prevented. Curiously, pure DMSO freezes at 58°F, a little below normal room temperature - well above the freezing point of water (32°F). But the freezing point of the mixture of the DMSO + water complexes goes as low as -200°F. Not surprisingly, water is the most common "impurity" in DMSO. A common test of purity is to check the freezing point. 99.9 percent DMSO freezes at 58°F, 99.5 percent DMSO at 40°F, and 99 percent DMSO resists until 10°F. A 70 percent solution remains liquid down to -110°F.

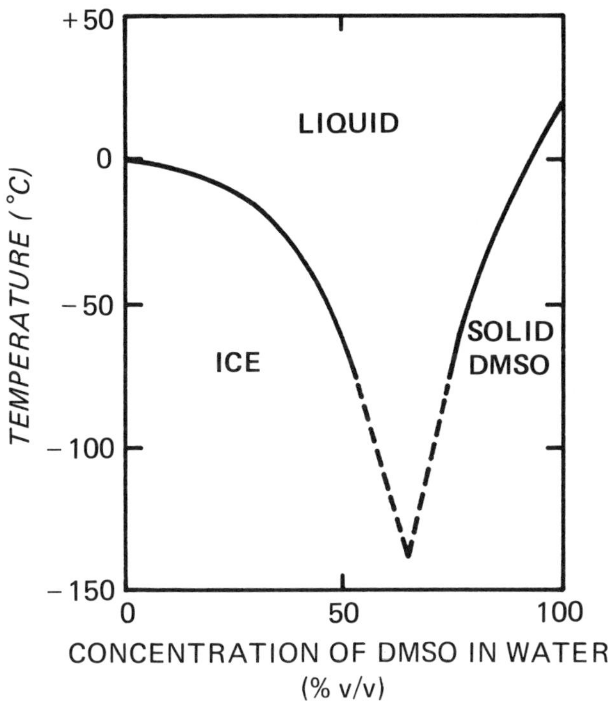

Pure water freezes at 32°F (O°C) and pure DMSO freezes at 64°F (18.5°C). However, the mixture of the two freezes well below these common temperatures. This phenomenon is undoubtedly one factor in the tremendous success of DMSO as a freeze protectant of living materials. This has become the most common use of DMSO in the biological laboratory at the moment. — A freeze test is one way to check purity and concentration of DMSO. 99+% DMSO will freeze in your normal refrigerator compartment, or out-of-doors on a chilly evening. DMSO does not decompose and is not at all damaged by repeated freezing and thawing.

Few people are aware that by far the most common biological application of DMSO is as an agent to protect living cells and tissues during freeze storage. The major uses are in preserving red blood cells and in storage of cattle sperm for future insemination. When thawed they are alive and regain full activity.

Of the over 7000 research reports on DMSO, at least half center on its ability as a freeze protector. Whenever there is a need in biological research to preserve cells or tissue samples for future examination and comparison, DMSO usually plays a part.

It is worth mentioning that the extensive research in this area includes a careful evaluation of the possible toxicity of DMSO. The general conclusion is that the toxicity of DMSO in these processes is negligible.

Under normal circumstances, water is intimately intertwined with most structures of the body. This is quite natural since water makes up over 75 percent of the volume of the body. When DMSO enters the body and begins to complex with water, one of the effects is to alter the place or position of water in many of the membranes. This can be expected to change the activity of the membranes - how they respond to their circumstances.

The relation to water also serves to explain the diuretic effect of DMSO. Diuretics increase the amount of urine and so tend to result in an overall removal of water from the body. Because DMSO moves preferentially into the blood and tends to attract water, the relative amount of water in the blood compared to the tissue actually increases. The kidneys attempt to balance water distribution. The result is a larger than normal output of urine.

The early hypothesis that DMSO reduces swelling (edema) through its action in attracting water (as an osmotic) is apparently false. The thought was that DMSO somehow pulled the water out of the swollen tissues into the blood.

How DMSO alters the movement of water in different portions of the body is more complex than was first imagined. For similar reasons the question of how DMSO works in minor burn therapy, reducing and preventing blisters and skin loss, is, again, up in the air. Current research should help to clarify matters.

2. DMSO is a Free Radical Scavenger

An early discovery about DMSO is its ability to protect cells against radiation damage. The importance of this discovery has been gradually unfolding since.

Radiation produces what are known as **free radicals** - and DMSO turns out to be a free radical scavenger. A little background explanation is needed to avoid the impression that this is a political drama over the development of nuclear reactors.

Very briefly, when cells, or anything containing some water, is exposed to a radioactive source, the radiation splits the water in a strange manner - producing free radicals ·H and ·OH.

If you have had a course in basic chemistry you will be familiar with the more common separation of molecules into ions, H^+, the hydrogen ion (which is the simplest acid), and OH- the hydroxyl ion (which is the simplest base or alkaline substance). These ion separations occur very frequently and the ions are not highly reactive - they don't mind being separated, even though the combined unit by itself normally has priority. Table salt, sodium chloride, separates into sodium ions and chloride ions when dissolved in water. Sodium is a positive ion and chloride is a negative ion.

Free radicals do not have ionic separation of charge - they are neutral. Being separated and neutral makes them highly reactive.

Free radicals have been described as the most powerfully destructive form of matter produced in biological systems. They react with anything and the result is usually destructive. They are very short-lived once produced because they react with whatever is available. The hydroxol free radicals - also referred to as **superoxides** - appear to be the most damaging to biological structures.

In a limited way, the body actually uses radicals to defend itself. Invading bacteria are ingested by special cells called phagocytes. Phagocytes produce a few radicals just for such appropriately destructive occasions. Once ingested, the bacteria is likely to be greeted with a free radical or two. One free radical properly placed is probably sufficient to destroy even a large bacterium.

The most recent research reveals that all oxygen consuming cells produce free radicals during normal activities. But they are rapidly eliminated by enzyme activity before cellular damage can occur. When stress or injury alter normal cellular processes, these radicals may be produced in such numbers that available enzymatic mechanisms are overwhelmed. The result is destruction of tissues, releasing toxins and escalating into a cyclic inflammatory episode: more toxins creating more destruction, releasing more toxins, creating more destruction, and so forth.

Our understanding of this most reactive form of matter has grown tremendously in the last five years. The most recent findings are summarized in **Superoxides**, edited by A.M. Michelson. It is this basic research that has given us clues to the mechanism by which DMSO has been providing therapeutic benefits.

Some researchers have put forth the hypothesis that all aging processes are the result of the actions of hydroxyl free radicals (superoxides). Your rate of aging is directly determined by the amount of superoxide your system produces. Others have suggested a general link to cancer.

So much for the bad news. The good news is that there are substances that react with free radicals so quickly that they serve to protect normal tissues. Such substances are known as "free radical scavengers." They are all anti-oxidants. By reacting with superoxides they prevent the free- wheeling, destructive oxidation of normal tissue. The most widely publicized free radical scavenger is Vitamin E. DMSO is probably more effective, at least in most situations, because of its ability to cross membranes.

Our understanding of the importance of free radical scavengers has come with our understanding of the mechanism of inflammation. Free radicals play a major role in the destructive cycle that escalates and perpetuates an

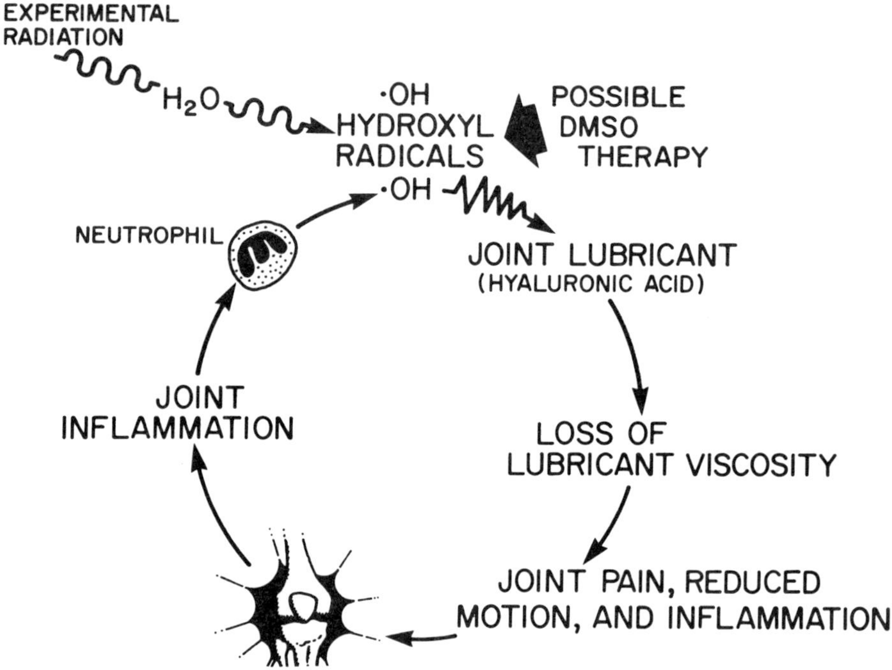

Experiments demonstrate that DMSO prevents the breakdown of hyaluronic acid, the body's main joint lubricant, by hydroxyl free readicals. The experiments used radiation to produce the hydroxyl radicals, but numerous other studies have established that neutrophils (a type of cell) in inflammed joints produce the same destructive radicals. By acting to protect the joint lubricant DMSO acts to break the inflammatory cycle.

inflammation. The free radical scavengers break the inflammatory cycle. We can see how this can occur directly, but recent studies in arthritis have shown an additional secondary mechanism.

DMSO and Free Radicals in Arthritis

What is destroyed in an inflammatory episode is not only cell and tissue structures but also important substances - such as joint lubricants. Researchers have recently demonstrated that DMSO protects joint lubricant from hydroxyl free radicals - over-abundant in inflamed joints. The benefit for the arthritis sufferer here is indirect. Without adequate joint lubricant, simple motion would produce additional stress, destruction and inflammation. This would accelerate the inflammatory process. By preventing the breakdown of the joint lubricant, DMSO de-escalates the inflammatory episode. This should shorten or decrease the severity of inflammatory arthritic attacks and significantly reduce long-term joint degeneration.

Although there is strong evidence that this process is taking place in DMSO therapy for arthritis, it is not yet clear how much benefit is actually achieved. It may only relieve 10 percent of the destruction of joint lubricant,

or only reduce inflammatory pressure by 10 percent or less. Human clinical trials are the ultimate test. What is perhaps most important about these advances and our understanding of the mechanisms is that clinical trials are possible without playing games about double-blind controls. It should be possible to monitor the rate of production and the amount of free radical present in a person's body at a particular time. The degree of breakdown in joint lubricant could also be determined. These physiological measures are more likely to convince skeptical physicians and patients than subjective reports about pain relief or difficult measures of degree of swelling inflammation or joint mobility.

Ironically, DMSO itself has been suggested as a method of measuring the presence of free radicals. The reaction of DMSO and free radicals is extremely rapid and complete and produces methane. The methane remains dissolved in the blood for a while and can be measured chemically.

Since the rate of free radical production can vary tremendously from person to person and from one period of your life to another, this may help to explain why a certain dosage of DMSO appears to produce dramatic benefits in some people, small long-term benefits in others, and for some, no benefits. Some people may well use up the DMSO much faster than others, sometimes before it reaches the place where it is most needed. Effective therapy for inflammatory problems using DMSO may require the physician to monitor the amount of DMSO (or methane) present in the blood a few hours after administration of a standard dose of DMSO.

Another popular theory to explain the action of DMSO as an anti-inflammatory has to do with its demonstrated ability to multiply the effect of cortisone between ten-fold and one thousand-fold. See the later discussion.

Special Note

Research reported in 1980-1981 clarifies and further substantiates earlier published reports showing that DMSO stabilizes and protects the all-important DNA molecule. DNA is the long string-like molecule in the nucleus of each cell that carries the chemically coded information responsible for directing cellular activity. DNA is also the hereditary material - containing the information on how to construct, as well as operate, any particular organism. A popular theory currently being tested is that most, if not all, aging and cancer occur because of damage to the DNA. The cells can repair some damage, but when the rate of damage exceeds the rate of repair, then aging occurs, or in localized regions, perhaps, the preliminary degeneration and cellular confusion leading to cancer.

DMSO protects the DNA from damage by hydroxyl free radicals (superoxides). One recent (1981) study showed that DMSO protected DNA 100 percent from damage by a free radical producer introduced into cells. Related experiments established that DMSO as a free radical scavenger provided 80 percent protection for DNA from gamma-radiation. (The other 20 percent damage is probably due to direct impact of radiation on the DNA.)

In high concentrations, DMSO also stabilizes DNA in the test-tube environment. This is partly by altering the action of water molecules normally associated with the DNA, and partly by changing the electrostatics (how the micro-electric charges interact) in the solutions. These two characteristics have earned DMSO a place in the research and development of recombinant-DNA (genetic engineering). How important these effects might be at the much lower concentration of DMSO likely to reach the nucleus of the cell in the body has yet to be determined.

3. The Very Special Solvent Properties

DMSO is one of a class of solvents that became available after WW II. A solvent is any liquid that dissolves other substances. Water is the best example. Other common solvents are alcohols, benzene, and acetone. An unexpected acceleration of certain chemical reactions occurs when DMSO is used in place of traditional solvents like water, alcohols, and acetone. The acceleration and increased efficiency of reactions occurring in DMSO had immediate commercial value.

It wasn't until the 1960's that the nature of DMSO-like solvents (bipolar, aprotic) became the subject of excited theoretical attention. Out of this analysis of the special effects produced by this new class of solvents, there came a better understanding of the whole picture of solvent participation in chemical reactions.

In other words, the rate at which a chemical transformation takes place - like from methanol to methane - depends on what the methanol and other reactants are dissolved in. Before the discovery and investigation of this new class of solvents, we understood very little about how the solvent itself could alter the rate, or even the direction of chemical reactions.

Because of the sensational acceleration of reaction rates the name "super solvents" was applied occasionally to describe this new class of solvents including DMSO and DMF (dimethyl formamide). Industrial applications are now numerous, and new valuable uses are still emerging every year or two.

Researchers have long anticipated that these special solvent characteristics are likely to be the basis for explaining many of the biological actions of DMSO. However, not all reactions are accelerated in DMSO; many are in fact retarded.

DMSO is a small molecule with dramatic electrostatic and magnetic configurations. For instance, the S-O bond is highly polar, like a miniature magnet (a north pole and a south pole). What effect this has in different circumstances is highly dependent on the circumstances. It is almost impossible to say DMSO does this or that **in general**. But we do know that it has major effects - one way or the other - on the electromagnetic characteristics of solutions.

DMSO frequently alters the often important effect of water in a reaction. Since water is the major substance in biological systems, much of what is said

in this section can be seen as an extension of the earlier discussion of the relation between DMSO and water.

Hypothesis and Limits of Our Understanding

Because of the highly circumstantial nature of the influence of DMSO, it is difficult to draw any conclusions from simple chemical evidence about what might happen in the complicated body-circumstance with the same chemicals. However, we know that DMSO may accelerate, by more than 100 times, a reaction with potassium ion (K^+) is substituted for sodium ion (Na^+). The reason appears to be that DMSO molecules fit around sodium ions - forming a sort of cocoon - more tightly than around potassium ions. The tighter the cocoon, the slower the reaction - at least under many circumstances. This particular feature appears to be the explanation - or at least a leading hypothesis - of the analgesic (pain relieving) characteristic of DMSO. An alternative hypothesis is that DMSO alters the action of an enzyme that is important to the membrane interplay of potassium and sodium ions.

Transmission of nerve impulses depends on the movement of sodium and potassium ions in certain proportions across the nerve cell membrane. It has been demonstrated that DMSO alters this exchange. The hypothesis is that this somehow accounts for the alleviation of pain. It may also be that the DMSO replaces water in the nerve cell membrane and thereby alters the normal properties crucial to maintaining the sodium/potassium balance. When membrane properties change, the sodium and potassium balance changes. This may well explain the blocking of pain impulses.

Broadly speaking the various solvent properties of DMSO probably account for its ability to penetrate the skin and cross membranes. However, attempts to be specific so far have failed to handle all the evidence. Much remains unexplained. The fact that DMSO dissolves both organic and inorganic substances has been suggested as a very general explanation. The skin may be thought of as having a double-barrier, one level repels oils and the other water-based salts. DMSO is able to pass both because it dissolves (and dissolves in) both types of substances.

The ability of DMSO to penetrate the skin has really been over-emphasized. Many other substances move across the skin quite easily. Water, alcohol and acetone all penetrate at rates close to or, in the case of acetone, exceeding the rate of DMSO. The value of DMSO as a vehicle is based more on its low toxicity and ability to dissolve a variety of other substances, rather than on its speed or ease of penetration.

Furthermore, DMSO will not carry just anything through the skin into the blood stream. Substances with a molecular weight above 3000 are greatly inhibited - this includes most fats, proteins, and carbohydrates. In fact, it excludes most medium size to larger substances in general. It will help some of these substances down into the second or third layers of skin, but this is not of any real significance (except for something like hydrocortisone, where it

may be helpful in treatment of certain skin problems). DMSO will not carry any bacteria through the skin into the blood. However, it will aid in the penetration of anti-perspirants, garden and household poisons, and so forth.

One condition where DMSO operates directly to dissolve something is in bursitis and perhaps in related cases where abnormal deposits are present. X-rays clearly show the gradual disappearance of a deposit. How DMSO actually accomplishes this is still not fully understood. Some investigators feel that a direct solvation process is too simple an explanation. Why DMSO would only dissolve the abnormal deposits is not explained. The structural chemistry of the abnormal deposits is known to be significantly different. Normal bone and cartilage are really alive - with their own blood supply and nerves. Simple deposits are just that - simple deposits. Once the deposit is removed the relief is essentially permanent, although reinjury of course remains a possibility.

4. The Influence on Enzyme Activity

The body produces two classes of protein: structural proteins and enzymatic proteins. Cells and tissues are composed of their own special structural proteins. Structural proteins are the basis of cellular architecture. Enzyme proteins, or enzymes, move around the body and serve as operators and activators. Enzymes participate in cellular activities - movement, digestion, repair, synthesis of other proteins, reproduction, and so forth.

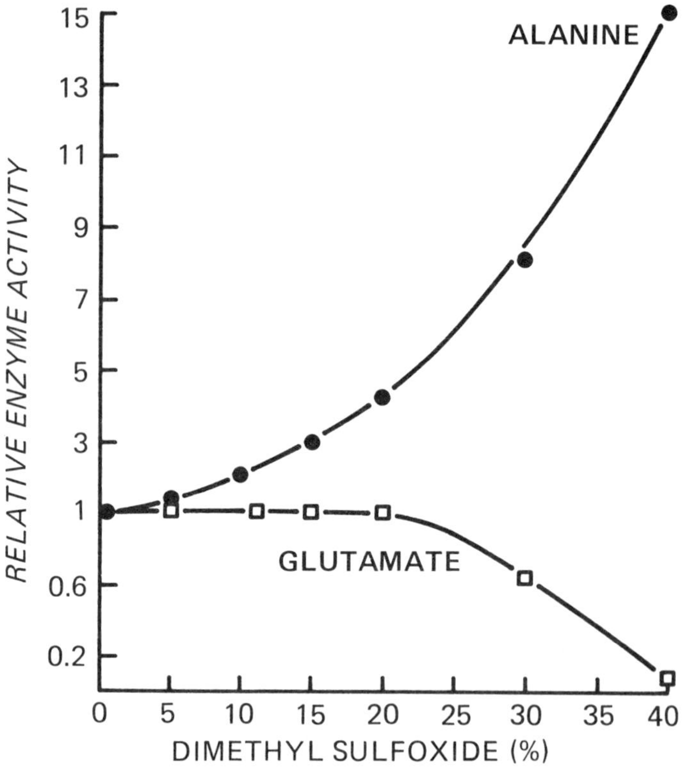

Water is often intimately connected to and involved in the structure of proteins.

Because of its strong tendency to bind to water, DMSO causes changes in a specific shape - twists and bends - of protein molecules. For enzymatic proteins, even slight changes in shape may result in significant changes in behavior and biochemical properties. Because enzymes are usually designed for highly specific purposes, the most common effect of the slight change in shape is to render the enzyme essentially inactive in the body.

Now enzymes and/or activities in the body are almost balanced, so that to inactivate one enzyme is to allow its opposite, balancing enzyme to be more active. Although DMSO probably serves only to slightly alter and thereby inhibit a few enzymes, the observed consequence may be the stimulation of another - the opposite enzyme or enzyme process.

One effect of DMSO on enzyme activity was noted quite early - it inhibits cholinesterase. This is a substance that breaks down one of the basic nerve transmitters - acetylcholine. Nerve transmitters are the chemical link between nerves.

The effects form a pattern: smooth muscle of the stomach increases in responsiveness, the diaphragm is less responsive, skeletal muscles tend to relax, and the threshold of stimulation of the vagus nerve is decreased by 50 percent. The overall effect would be to stimulate what is referred to as the parasympathetic division of the nervous system.

However, evaluating the effects in this first system has been complicated by an overlay pattern due to the interplay of DMSO with special physiological activating substances called prostaglandins. Only within the last five years has the action of DMSO on prostaglandin activity been clearly established by researchers. But this may account for some of the earliest observed effects of DMSO.

Briefly, DMSO seems to inhibit some prostanglandins and through this action to enhance the effects of others. The most obvious consequences are the improvement of blood flow and the reduction of microcirculation clogging around injured tissues. DMSO lessens the stickiness of cellular debris that block through-flow and cause swelling in the first place.

The therapeutic result is seen, for instance, where DMSO reduces the swelling and facilitates the healing of a blackeye. Return to normal occurs in one-half to one-third the regular time. Blood flow is improved first by stimulation of the capillaries to contract - reducing swelling.

Red blood cells tend to form blood clots because they become sticky whenever there is bleeding due to injury in some area of the body. DMSO inhibits this tendency to become sticky and so produces a slight temporary increase in the measured time it takes the normal blood to clot naturally. (This is not grounds for worrying about bleeding; the change is in terms of a few seconds.) This undoubtedly helps to account for the clearing of the clogged microcirculation after an injury - aiding in the healing process.

Another important application is in the treatment of stroke where in animals DMSO has operated to prevent the typical increase in the size of the blocking embolism (blood clot). More important in stroke is another prostaglandin effect: the apparent stimulation of the collateral circulation (secondary or back-up system). The effect, at least in animals, is to prevent

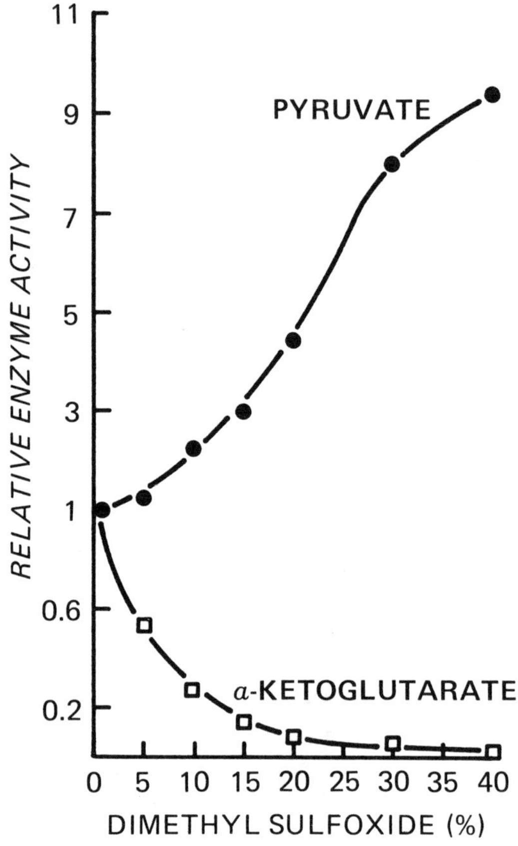

brain damage and the residual loss of mental and physical capabilities. If this turns out to work as well in humans, it will undoubtedly be the most important application of DMSO so far discovered.

Another effect of DMSO, observed early, but only recently understood, again is traceable to improved blood flow. This is the ability of DMSO to greatly increase the effects of a normal dosage of another drug. Insulin, tranquilizers, steroids, barbiturates, alcohol, anti-fungal agents, antibiotics, digitoxin (digitalis) - all have more pronounced effect in their biological actions when mixed with DMSO. Two hypotheses have dominated in the attempts to explain this effect. One, again, traces back to the effect of DMSO on water bonds. Cortisone, for instance, reaches the position in the membranes where it is most effective because DMSO alters the membrane structure when it links to the water in the membrane. However, most of the effects appear to be due simply to the improved blood flow. DMSO aids the delivery of the drugs throughout the body.

5. Stimulation Toward Maturity

One last grouping of biological effects should be mentioned here. DMSO appears to stimulate cellular activity in general. One hypothesis attributes this to alteration of the action of some other prostaglandins. Another hypothesis suggests action to stimulate hormone production. These seem to be developing towards one hypothesis where the action on prostaglandins has an effect on hormone manufacture. In one form of leukemia (cancer of the blood cells), the problem is that the blood cells never mature. The body responds to the lack of mature blood cells by manufacturing more and more new immature blood cells. The result is a massive overabundance of immature blood cells. By accident it was found that DMSO stimulates the blood cells to develop to maturity. Several hundred research papers have been published in this area of inquiry since first discovered in 1971.

Another, perhaps related, line of research involves stimulation (and/or inhibition) of certain activities of the immune system. Current research hopes to find an application to auto-immune disorders such as myasthenia gravis, multiple sclerosis, lupus, and rheumatoid arthritis. Normally, the immune system attacks and rejects foreign matter that has entered the body. In auto-immune disorders there is confusion and the immune system attacks self-substances natural to the body. DMSO may stop the auto-immune attack by inhibiting something, or may stimulate the immune system's cells to greater maturity and greater ability to distinguish foreign from self-substances.

Comment: Whatever else is said about DMSO and whatever its final place in treatment, it is clear that much of the research on DMSO and its actions in the body has led us to important advances in our understanding of how the body is put together and performs its diverse functions.

How Is DMSO Metabolized?

Absorption Through the Skin

DMSO in solution with water is rapidly absorbed through the skin (some in seconds, most in minutes). The rate of penetration is greatest for a 90 percent DMSO solution. However, the rate between 70 percent - 90 percent is about the same. As a result, most of the clinical experience with DMSO is in this 70 percent - 90 percent concentration range. Lower concentrations (15 percent - 50 percent) are employed when the solution is applied to mucous membranes, the body's naturally wet surfaces: bladder, anus, mouth and gums, sinuses, eyes, and so forth.

Distribution Throughout the Body

Once applied to any area, DMSO disperses gradually throughout the body. Thirty minutes after administration more than half (60 percent - 85 percent) remains in the tissues at the site of application. After one hour only 11 percent - 19 percent remains at the site. After 24 hours whole body distribution is complete.

DMSO distributes preferentially to those areas where there is the most water. More ends up in the blood than in the organs and tissues, and least in the bones. When DMSO is applied to the skin, the amount in the blood slowly increases to a maximum after about two to four hours.

Biological Processing in the Body (Metabolism)

The body processes DMSO in either one of two opposite directions: adding or removing an atom of oxygen. Adding an oxygen atom (oxidation) produces dimethyl sulfone ($DMSO_2$). Removing an oxygen atom (reduction) produces dimethyl sulfide (DMS).

When DMS alone is administered to the body both DMSO and $DMSO_2$ are produced in the processing. However, when $DMSO_2$ is administered, neither DMSO or DMS are detected. This is summarized by the arrows between the substances in the diagram.

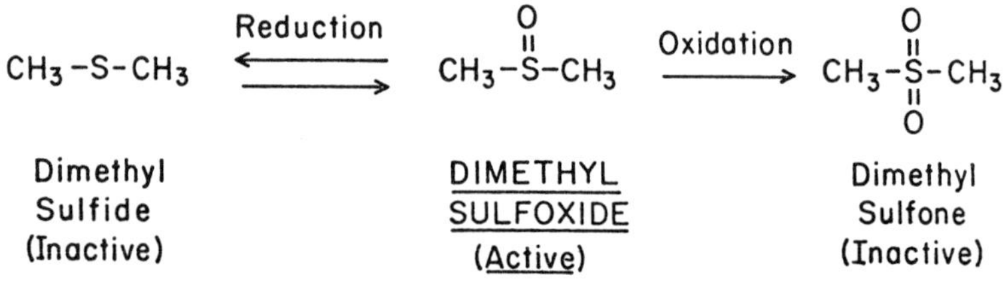

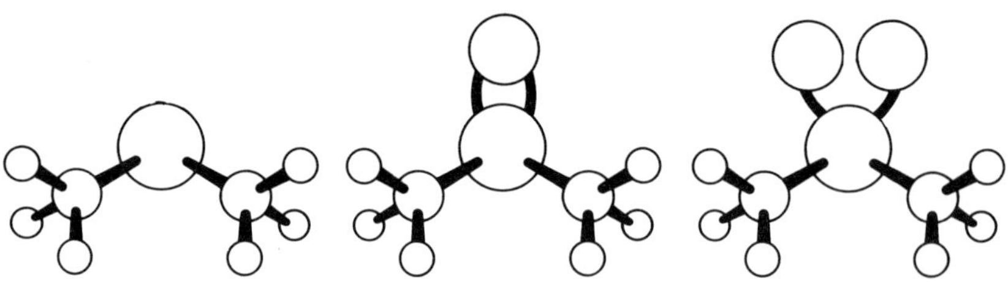

DMS DMSO $DMSO_2$

Up to half a dose of DMSO has been measured, unchanged, excreted in the urine over a period of 20 days. However, both basic research and clinical studies indicate that the rate and particular proportions eventually expelled as DMS, DMSO or $DMSO_2$ may vary significantly.

It is hypothesized that the variance observed here may be a clue to the fact that some people respond sooner or not at all to some dosage levels of DMSO. In brief, there may be important different levels of biosubstances essential to DMSO processing in different people's bodies. For instance, diet (what, how much, how often) and exercise may alter the specific rates and proportions of DMS and $DMSO_2$ in processing DMSO.

It is worth emphasizing that DMSO metabolism is surprisingly simple. Little or no DMSO appears to become involved in other more complex biochemical pathways, where, for instance, sulfur containing substances are otherwise often found. DMSO operates at a fairly primitive level in terms of chemical reactions, although the effects themselves may be sophisticated and complex.

About five percent of the DMSO entering the body is eventually removed as DMS. When associated with the body, DMS is a gas, because its boiling temperature, $98^oF.$, is just below normal body temperature, 98.6^oF. DMS comes off the lungs with normal exchange of gases, like carbon dioxide, CO_2, and is exhaled.

A large portion of DMSO entering the body is slowly oxidized into dimethyl sulfone, $DMSO_2$. The level of $DMSO_2$ peaks between 36 - 72 hours after administering DMSO. The dimethyl sulfone is extremely stable and leaves the body unchanged, primarily through the urine.

The overall processing of DMSO by the body is really rather fast. Within 24 hours 90-95 percent of the DMSO from a single application is metabolized. This means it is either changed to DMS and exhaled, or expelled in the urine, unchanged, or having been changed to $DMSO_2$. The DMSO level in the blood is only one-half its peak (at 2-4 hours) after 6-8 hours. All traces of DMSO are gone after 12 days, whereas dimethyl sulfone is detectable for up to 20 days.

Properties of the Sulfide and Sulfone

Dimethyl sulfide (DMS) is a stable compound. At room temperature (72^oF) it's a liquid. At body temperature (98.6^oF) it's a gas. Many clinical reports refer to DMS as a source of the sulfurous, garlic, onion-like, or oysterish odor of the breath of patients receiving DMSO. But it is only a part of the odor. Dimethyl sulfide, when ultrapure, possesses a not unpleasant, penetrating ether-like odor. It serves in industry as an odor enhancer and is critical to the fresh odor of seafoods, vegetables, milk, coffee, and tea.

Dimethyl sulfone ($DMSO_2$) is a stable, odorless compound. Although it is very soluble in warm water, it is only slightly soluble in cold water. The exceptional chemical stability of $DMSO_2$ possibly accounts for its long-term residence in the blood after a single dose of DMSO, and its excretion unchanged.

3

GENERAL QUESTIONS OF TOXICITY

Since all chemical compounds have toxicity to some degree, it is appropriate that we briefly review the basis for the evaluation of toxicity. Toxicology is the science of determining lethal and unwholesome effects of a drug. This includes looking at both local effects and possible derangements of whole systems of otherwise normal activity.

These studies can be further pursued to see whether the changes can reverse themselves naturally, or with cessation of medication, or by use of some additional corrective therapy. Since there are several conditions where long-term use of DMSO may be beneficial, possible long-term toxic effects that may not be apparent for occasional or short-term application must also be considered. (One or two martinis a day may actually be beneficial, both in the short term and long term, whereas six or seven a day may well lead to cumulative liver damage.)

Because DMSO is often applied topically, and can carry other substances through the skin, there is a special question of toxicity here peculiar to DMSO (and similar substances). This is referred to as "vehicle toxicity" since DMSO acts as a vehicle for other possible toxins.

Immediate and Short-Term Toxicity

As compared to all other medications, DMSO is of relatively low immediate and short-term toxicity. Generally speaking, the amount of DMSO that it would take to kill a person in a single dose is about the same as for drinking alcohol. This is true regardless of the concentration for both DMSO and drinking alcohol. The faster it is taken, of course, the greater likelihood of a lethal reaction.

For massive single doses, the conclusion drawn in 1971, based on a review of the numerous, wide-ranging animal studies completed at that time, still holds: regardless of how high the dose given, and regardless of the route of administration, if the animal survived for 24 hours, all signs and symptoms of toxicity eventually disappeared. The ability of DMSO to be absorbed and spread through the body rapidly is so great that, as far as can be determined, there is no increase in toxicity with repeated daily doses over short periods (2-7 days).

A short-term (14-day) carefully controlled study of toxicity in 100 humans involving topical application of 1 gram of DMSO per kilogram of body weight per day (about 1/2 cup of 80% DMSO gel per day) produced **no toxicity**. Physical exams, blood tests, urine analyses and complete eye and visual examinations were undertaken before, during and after the DMSO treatment period. There were no changes in laboratory values, and no changes in any way suggestive of an abnormal refractive index characteristic of the eye changes observed in some lower animals.

The National Academy of Sciences conducted an extensive review of DMSO toxicity in 1974. As they point out, the only toxicity worth mentioning occurs from large doses of high concentration DMSO - particularly if taken orally or given intravenously.

> "Compared to most drugs or commonly recognized toxic agents, DMSO is relatively impotent on a weight or molar dosage basis. The compound is not innocuous, however, especially when administered at high concentrations (greater than 50%) and can give rise to serious, acute, toxic reactions. For instance, if such concentrations are given **intravenously**, hemolysis (break- down of red blood cells) will result, leading to hemoglobin in the urine, anemia, pulmonary obstruction, and edema, hemorrhage, hypertension, etc. Large doses of high concentrations of DMSO **orally** produce gastroenteritis and bowel hemorrhage, or when given by other routes, produce analogous toxic effects appropriate to the avenue of administration."

The wording here may appear a little strong. For perspective, it should be noted that an almost identical statement could be made about the toxicity of large doses of high concentration ethanol (drinking alcohol).

Only high concentrations of DMSO administered intravenously or orally in large quantities are singled out for special mention. Later studies of intravenous DMSO indicate that 10-20% concentrations are not toxic, even though there is still some red blood cell breakdown. DMSO apears to protect the body from the normal, expected toxic effects of red blood cell breakdown.

Intermediate Term Toxicity

Aside from the question of eye toxicity in lower animals, there is no additional toxicity for daily doses of DMSO for periods up to 90 days.

A variety of toxic effects have been recorded for animals receiving large repeated doses of DMSO for periods of months. However, almost all these reports are associated with studies of repeated intravenous infusions of high concentrations (40%-80%) of DMSO.

An intermediate term (90 day), carefully controlled study of toxicity in 66 humans involving topical application of one gram of DMSO per kilogram of body weight per day (about 1/2 cup of 80% DMSO gel per day) produced **no toxicity**. Physical exams, blood tests, urine analysis and complete eye and visual examinations were undertaken before, during and after the DMSO treatment period. The subjects in this study were all different from those in the 14-day study. Both studies were undertaken on a male prison population (State Prison Hospital at Vacaville, California, October 1967 through February 1968).

As in the previously mentioned 14-day study, no significant abnormalities were observed in the large battery of blood chemistries, peripheral blood and urine analyses. Physical examinations, including blood pressure, pulse, temperature and respiratory rate, examination of the neck and thyroid, lungs, heart, liver, kidney, spleen, abdomen, genitourinary system, rectum and extremities, and an ear, nose and throat, and neurological examination, showed no significant difference between subjects receiving DMSO and the control group. Likewise, the extensive opthalmological examinations were unable to detect changes in any way suggestive of an abnormal refractive index, characteristic of the eye changes observed in some lower animals.

To quote the director of the two (14-day and 90 day) studies, Dr. Richard D. Brobyn: "A very extensive study of DMSO was conducted at 3 to 30 times the usual treatment dosage in humans, for three months. DMSO appears to be a very safe drug for human administration, and in particular, the lens changes that occur in certain mammalian species do not occur in man under this very high, prolonged treatment regimen. I am very glad to be able to present these data at this time, so that we can permanently dispel the myth that DMSO is in any way a toxic or dangerous drug."

Long Term Toxicity

The question of possible toxicity due to long-term use is problematic for virtually all modern pharmaceutical products. It is simply not feasible to test drugs for periods of 50-75 years before using them.

Certain tests can be done, however, that give us a fair idea of whether it is reasonable to expect any long-term toxicity. One test is whether the drug tends to accumulate in the body with repeated doses. If it did, then one might expect toxic consequences to appear only once the amount in the body reached

a certain level.

DMSO does not tend to accumulate in the tissues. A single dose is almost all cleared from the body within 24 hours. However, of course, if one were to repeat the dose prior to complete clearance, there would be a build-up of dosage.

Absolutely complete clearance of DMSO and its metabolites (DMS and $DMSO_2$) may take up to three weeks.

Anyone using DMSO very regularly might be well advised to exercise added precaution by adopting the "5 day on, 2 day off" regimen recommended by various physicians. And at least once a year stop all usage for 4-6 weeks. If there is any long-term toxicity, this procedure may lessen the likelihood of its turning up. Particularly with a 4-6 week pause, the body should have a sure chance to clear out all DMSO and heal any area of otherwise hidden damage.

Another way to explore the possibility of toxicity from long-term use is through experimental examination of the toxicity of larger dosages for somewhat shorter periods. The side effects of DMSO are definitely dose related: the more DMSO in high concentration, the greater the side effects. Again, except for the possible eye toxicity, several species, including monkeys, have received very large dosages of DMSO for periods up to 1 year without any detectable toxicity.

A third way to check, now, for possible long-term effects is to undertake retrospective evaluations. This involves finding and examining patients months and years after their use of DMSO, or where they may have been using it regularly over the years. Prisoners in the two Vacaville toxicity studies were given follow-up exams at varying periods up to one year after treatment was discontinued. No toxicity was detected; in particular, complete eye examinations revealed no significant ocular changes.

When eye changes first turned up in lower mammals in 1965, no reports of eye problems had been reported for any of the several million humans who had used DMSO. Drs. Jacob and Rosenbaum, in Portland, Oregon, had 32 patients examined by opthalmologists connected with the University of Oregon Medical School. These had been treated from 3 to 19 months at an average dose of 30 grams of DMSO per day (1/4 cup of 80% DMSO). None of these showed any of the characteristic lens changes that had been seen in animals.

One patient in Seattle was thoroughly checked. He had, by chance, had a complete pre-treatment examination performed by an opthalmologist several months prior to his neck injury. He was 19 years old, and at the date of his post treatment exam, he had received 60 grams of DMSO per day for 20 months. His follow-up exam was completely normal.

During 1966, the pharmaceutical companies continued to collect case reports and no real toxicity of any kind was being observed. Merck and Company collected 17,000 case reports, Syntex collected approximately 7,000, and E.R. Squibb and Sons around 3,000. These well-documented trials and retrospective checks for long-term problems have all been negative

concerning any medium to long range toxicity.

Monkey studies, both in Germany and the U.S. in the 1960's, observed no lens changes at 11 grams of DMSO per kilogram of body weight administered topically, and 5 grams of DMSO per kilogram of body weight orally per day after one year.

The conclusion was that the lens changes were species-specific, and that the primate was probably much more resistant than other mammals.

After 18 years of clinical use by an estimated ten million persons around the world, not one well-documented case of serious toxicity due to DMSO has been reported, aside from the inevitable, occasional hypersensitivity reaction.

The Question of Eye Toxicity: A History

On November 11, 1965, clinical research on DMSO in the United States was terminated by the Food and Drug Administration. A conference between the FDA and the pharmaceutical companies who were involved in the research was called because lens changes had been observed in a number of mammalian species. No changes had been recorded in man or any primates. Many felt that the FDA was overreacting. But because there had been no pretreatment examinations of eyes and a large number of patients were under therapy, the pharmaceutical companies agreed to discontinue, temporarily, human clinical trials.

Monkey studies completed in 1966 reported no changes at very high doses administered daily for a full year. A retrospec tive eye examination was performed on a number of patients who had been regular users for up to two and a half years. No abnormalities could be detected. It was becoming increasingly clear that these lens changes were probably species-specific, and that the primate (including man) was probably much more resistant than other mammals.

In December of 1966, the FDA permitted the resumption of clinical testing of DMSO, but only for serious conditions for which no satisfactory therapy was available.

In January, 1967, Dr. Richard Brobyn was retained as a consultant at E.R. Squibb and Sons to develop a program to re-establish full scale clinical research on DMSO. The Food and Drug Administration, at the same time, had planned a short-term study to evaluate only the lens problem. They agreed, after a consultation with E.R. Squibb and Sons, to include their study as a part of a more complete study of human toxicity. This led to two closely related studies.

The short-term (14 day) study was conducted at the State Prison Hospital at Vacaville, California in October of 1967. The long-term (90 day) study was conducted at the same institution from November 21, 1967 to February 20,

1968. Several careful and detailed studies of the actual lens changes in lower animals were also completed between 1966 and 1968.

On the basis of the results of these animal and human studies, the FDA further relaxed its restrictions on human clinical testing in 1968. They allowed clinical trials with DMSO for several more medical conditions - but only for periods of 14 days or less. Extensive reports were required, but the stipulation that physicians obtain FDA approval prior to administering the drug was dropped.

During 1970, testing was gradually opened further, based upon evaluation of individual applications. Such testing normally requires a specific license from the FDA, obtained through a proposal outlining the procedures. Over the years, the FDA has abandoned its requirements for ongoing eye examinations for anyone involved in an experimental program using DMSO. Nothing has ever shown up, not even the subtle preliminary changes detectable fairly early in some animals.

It should also be noted that the FDA - the Veterinary Branch - approved DMSO for use in animals in 1971, and it is widely and successfully used in veterinary medicine. This approval and this current use occur in full awareness of the clear and repeated demonstration that DMSO in relatively large and repeated doses will cause lens changes in dogs, rabbits, and swine.

This practice, of approving a drug with known toxicity, is by no means exceptional in the case of DMSO. Most drugs used by physicians and veterinarians have been shown to have some one or several serious toxic consequences in large doses. Even today, for instance, aspirin is a leading cause of kidney failure in heavy aspirin users.

Despite the numerous experiments and clinical evaluations and the complete absence of reports of lens changes from any of the millions of humans who have used DMSO - many for over 15 years regularly - the question still remains open as to whether regular long-term use of DMSO in relatively large doses might produce some lens changes in humans.

Since it is clear that the phenomenon is dose-related, those persons just starting to use DMSO in the 1980's have a good chance of being alerted of any possible changes - from those already long-term users, early enough to stop or cutdown use. But the final evaluation of danger must involve an understanding of the nature and seriousness of the changes if they were to occur. Keep in mind that the potential toxicity of DMSO is not life-threatening as is kidney failure associated with heavy, long-term use of aspirin. Obviously, in all cases, the physician and/or the patient must make a judgment concerning values, whether the benefits of a particular therapy are worth the long-term risks of serious toxicity.

The nature of the lens change

The effect of repeated doses of DMSO on the eyes of laboratory animals has been well-documented and often repeated. The effect is unique; no other compound has been reported to cause even a similar effect.

The mechanism appears to be indirect. Direct applications to the eyes of animals did not accelerate the phenomenon. There is some evidence that DMSO taken orally is somewhat more likely to produce the change than when applied topically application to the skin. This has lead to the hypothesis that the mechanism involves disturbance of some chemical, metabolic process. Accordingly, it is suspected that the changes occur not as a result of DMSO directly, but as a result of some secondary substance produced when the (unknown) metabolic process is disturbed.

We also know that the change is dose-related. The higher the dose, and the more often it is administered, the greater the likelihood of the lens change occurring. All our knowledge of the lens change is from animal studies. Effects similar to those seen in animals have not been observed in man.

Technically Speaking

Technically speaking, the cortical fibers of the lens become less relucent (light-reflecting) than normal. The relucence of the deeper cortical fibers and lens nucleus remains unchanged. The result is the creation of a more convex refracting surface, which is further back than the usual refracting surface (the anterior lens capsule). The effect on the visual mechanics in laboratory animals is the production of myopia (near-sightedness), and the myopic error becomes more severe with longer administration or exposure to higher concentrations of DMSO. The clinical appearance in some of the more severely affected animals is that of pearl-like opalescence of the center of the lens. In some cases, the center of the lens looks opaque, though it is actually quite clear.

The myopia appears to involve a change in the density of the material that makes up the lens. The refractive index - a measure of how much a clear material tends to bend light passing through it - decreases. In one of the dog studies, it was reported that every instance of nucleur haze was preceded by marked myopic changes by at least one month. It is still unknown whether or not the visible changes will occur if DMSO treatment is suspended after myopia has developed. However, considering the dose-drive, further development is not likely once DMSO treatments are stopped.

Don Wood, the researcher who looked into the changes most carefully, feels that changes in refractive index might be explained by the loss of soluble lens protein with a corresponding increase in the insoluble components. Although the conjectures have been made as to hypothetical mechanisms, no simple explanation for the lens change has been forthcoming.

The lenticular effect has been produced by the application of DMSO to the skin of rabbits at a dosage of 1 gram per kilogram of body weight per day over a period of 11 weeks, in dogs at a dosage of 2.5 grams/kilograms per day for 9 weeks, and in swine at a dosage of 1.5 grams/kilograms per day for 16 weeks. Higher doses produce lenticular changes in a shorter time. It has been reported that no effect was produced in rabbits given 0.5 grams/kilograms per day cutaneously for 30 days. In one study of dogs, no lenticular effects were

produced at a dosage of 1 gram/kilogram per day, given orally for 1 year.

In other species, the effect of DMSO on the lens is equivocal. Changes were reported in the lens of rats given 9 grams/kilograms per day after 24 weeks. In another study in which the same dose rate was used, no changes were seen after 2 years. Lower doses have not produced lenticular changes. No changes were observed in horses administered 0.4 grams/kilograms per day cutaneously for 14 days. In horses given 90% DMSO at approximately 0.6 grams/kilograms per day for about 2 months, however, there appeared to be a small change in the static refraction towards myopia. Whether this change is significant cannot be determined with certainty, because of the design of the investigation.

The lenticular effect is not well defined in monkeys. No changes were detected in young monkeys that were given DMSO at doses up to 9 grams/kilogram per day, orally or cutaneously, for 18 months. Other investigators detected slight lenticular changes (myopia) within 14 weeks in monkeys that were administered 9 grams/kilogram per day, and changes were suspected in those receiving 3 grams/kilogram per day.

Once established, the changes persist for a long time. To date, no reports of complete disappearance have been seen, however, regression of the lens change has been reported in swine.

THE HUMAN EYE STUDIES

Dr. Frank Hull was the opthalmologist in charge during the human toxicity studies at the State Prison Hospital at Vacaville, California. He reported the opthalmological findings obtained in the study of human volunteers treated dermally with 1 gram/kilogram DMSO daily for 12 weeks.

Thirty-eight treated and 18 control patients were evaluated for accommodation, near point of convergence, ocular tension, refraction, visual acuity, biomicroscopy, opthalmoscopy, pupillary mydriasis and peripheral and central visual field examinations. Treatment failed to show any changes in the parameters described above. Patients were also examined at varying periods up to 1 year after treatment was discontinued. The follow-up examinations likewise revealed no significant ocular changes.

Finally, the more immediate question must be considered. If changes were to occur in my eyes, how would this alter my vision? And would the change be correctable with glasses?

One reviewer comments, "It is noteworthy that in none of the reports on eye changes was there mention of alteration in visual acuity of the subject. Dogs never showed difficulty in running, jumping or avoiding obstacles, despite a marked change in the lens refraction."

However, unpublished communications from two researchers involved in Wood's careful rabbit studies suggested that there was no doubt in their minds that in severe cases, vision is noticeably impaired. The fact that this was not documented did not alter their opinion in the slightest.

DMSO as a Limited Vehicle for Toxins

Because DMSO is often applied topically (to the skin surface) and can carry other substances through the skin with it, there is a special problem of potential toxicity here. This problem is not, in fact, unique to DMSO. Other skin-penetrating solvents, such as water, alcohol, and acetone, have the same sort of toxic potential.

Most people are unaware of the almost equivalent danger of water-dissolved and DMSO-dissolved substances penetrating the skin. The difference with DMSO is only its ability to dissolve some toxic substances that water doesn't, and in some cases DMSO will carry substances through the skin faster. It is important to keep in mind that most substances that pass through the skin with DMSO (or with other solvents), can pass through the skin on their own. Even a dry powder can dissolve in skin surface moisture and pass through the skin.

The ability of substances mixed with DMSO to penetrate the skin more easily than otherwise has been evaluated for a fairly wide range of chemical materials. We can say at least that small, nonionized (i.e., excluding salts) molecules of low molecular weight are transported through the skin with DMSO. Large substances of high molecular weight such as insulin are not passed through the skin to any significant extent.

The longer any substance is on the skin surface the more likely it will penetrate. The DMSO has been shown to pass through the skin 100 times faster than some substances it has been mixed with. This observation has led to the hypothesis that DMSO, in many instances, simply creates passages through the skin. This may occur through the mechanism of DMSO replacing water in protein-water complexes in the skin. The proteins - and therefore the protein-barrier of the skin - changes its shape, twisting slightly in odd places, creating channels or passages. The process is entirely reversible and the permeability (openness to penetration by small molecules) lasts, at most, a few hours.

It is likely that acetone and alcohol have similar ways of altering skin structure. And we have probably all experienced the effects of prolonged exposure of the skin to water (wetness, dampness, etc.). It is worth noting, also, that occlusive patches or any procedure that cuts the skin off from fairly free exposure to the air, will result in much greater permeability. Occlusive patches are, in fact, a recent addition to common procedures for administering a medication. Occlusive patches are now manufactured with the medication imbedded in them. The drug slowly diffuses into and through the skin under the patch.

The main point of all this is that the vehicle toxicity potential of DMSO is not really as extraordinary as it has sometimes been represented to be. When one is exposed to toxic substances in the environment, one should be extremely careful. For instance, the danger of inhaling or swallowing a certain amount of a garden insecticide is much greater than having it penetrate through your skin - whether you have been using DMSO or not.

However, if you are using DMSO, it is defintely worth taking extra precautions.

Precautions Based on Vehicle Toxicity

1. Avoid bringing anything into contact with the area where the DMSO has been applied for at least 30 minutes after initial application.

2. For up to three hours extra precautions should be taken in handling any toxic chemicals: household cleaning agents, hair dyes, clothes dyes, garden or household pesticides, and so forth.

During the initial period, **the main potential danger is from the wet surface coming into contact** with clothes and fabrics or furniture containing dyes. Painted objects, magazines, newspapers, and so forth contain substances that could be taken up onto DMSO-wet hands. Once finished with letting the DMSO absorb through your skin (15-30 minutes), wipe off any remaining wetness. You then enter the second period of up to 3 (some say 4) hours. Here, the main point is simply to **avoid prolonged direct contact** with any toxic substances. The potential danger is limited to the area where you applied the DMSO. There is no alteration in general skin permeability - in areas where DMSO has not been applied.

According to many people familiar with the properties of DMSO, all this is really being super-cautious. Certainly the amount of toxin penetrating the skin in most cases is likely to be so miniscule that concern with dangers is questionable. The only real danger, according to this line of thinking, is with some form of regular abuse.

Furthermore, since it will take several minutes (up to an hour) for significant amounts of most toxins to penetrate even DMSO-treated skin, there is a rather simple solution. If, after having treated an area of skin with DMSO it does come in contact with some toxic substance - **wash the toxin off**. Since this should be a normal, natural response to exposure to any poison, there may be only a very little extra concern when using DMSO. Penetration of toxins also takes time. Don't panic if you spill a bottle of pesticide on your DMSO-treated hands - just wash it off (promptly).

Most of us apply anti-perspirants, lotions, powders and cosmetics to various areas of our body. These substances deserve special attention because they remain on the body surface for long periods. If applying DMSO to a shoulder, one should not use an anti-perspirant that day under that arm. DMSO has been demonstrated to enhance the penetration of these substances, as well as cosmetic products. Do not apply them over areas where you have applied DMSO that day (or at least not for 6-8 hours).

Skin lotions pose less of a danger. Something like Vaseline Intensive Care Lotion can be applied to a DMSO-treated area without (any known) danger. For those who experience a skin rash, this sort of medicated lotion is not only permitted, but is commonly recommended by physicians.

For those who must work around toxic substances, normal clothing or gloves should be adequate protection. If in doubt, ask whether the poisons are likely to penetrate the clothing or gloves.

Precautions and Warnings

Warnings: The Greatest Dangers

The Food and Drug Administration required a brief entry on the package insert under **Warnings** on the approved Research Industries DMSO product, RIMSO-50. (An identical entry is on the RIMSO-70 (70% DMSO) package insert, having received preliminary approval for human testing.)

The entry begins by referring to an early study that demonstrated DMSO can initiate the release of histamine.

Histamine is a substance present in virtually all skin cells. Release of histamine is a common response to local injury or irritation. It is the histamine (rather than the injury or the irritant) that typically produces the "wheal and flare reaction" (inflammation, slight hardened swelling and reddish area). This is the most visible part of the body's standard response to minor injury or irritation. Everyone is familiar with the use of anti-histamines to reduce the symptoms of minor irritation due to a cold. In the nasal-sinus area, release of histamine results in a stuffy nose. From the clinical trials it is safe to conclude that DMSO is a minor irritant for some people some of the time.

Inflammatory or Anti-Inflammatory

There is a possible confusion here. DMSO is renowned as an anti-inflammatory - the opposite of an irritant. But it does have this side effect for about 1 in 4 people of producing minor irritation. If DMSO were primarily an irritant, it would not make sense to use it to reduce inflammation. In fact, it is quite effective in reducing sinus irritation (sinusitis) - like an anti-histamine (although probably by a different mechanism of action). The point of mentioning all of this is clarified by the next entry on the approved package insert.

Perspective on Super-Allergic Reactions

It is generally accepted by the medical community that almost every substance known to man will produce a super-allergic reaction in someone, somewhere, sometime. The second entry on the package insert states that there has been an occasional hypersensitivity reaction with topical DMSO administration.

Following this is the standard advice that if super-allergic symptoms (known as anaphylactoid symptoms) develop, one should institute appropriate therapy. For the average person, this means one should call an ambulance - or reach a physician as soon as possible. Both are equipped with materials to give an injection (usually adrenalin).

It must be emphasized that this sort of reaction is extremely rare, and furthermore, there is little, if any, reason to expect a reaction more from DMSO than from other substances in the world.

Intermediate Allergic-Type Reactions

With topical administration of 90% - 100% DMSO, there is apparently a slight chance of an intermediate allergic-type reaction. The next entry under warnings refers to the occurrence of three cases among approximately 2,000 patients: "acute generalized urticaria that could be reasonably attributed to the drug were reported." The term "acute" means that it happens rapidly rather than over a long period. Generalized urticaria is known more commonly among non-professionals as hives. This is a condition marked by large reddish blotches on the skin - like the histamine "wheal and flare." It can be localized, one blotch, or generalized, with many. The entry finally notes that two of the three cases complained of shortness of breath, and one had some swelling of the larynx. These are common symptoms associated with acute generalized urticaria.

Although it is important that anyone using any drug should be aware of the possibility of severe as well as intermediate and minor allergic reactions, most physicians agree that these isolated negative reactions are so rare and, where intermediate, minor. They are not life-threatening, that they should not detract from the responsible use of drugs as therapeutic agents.

Since most patients never read package inserts, they are usually unaware of even the slight danger of an allergic reaction to any drug. As compared to the many other chemical substances - foods, drugs, cosmetics, cleansing agents, pollens, etc. - there is no reason to believe DMSO is more likely to cause any serious allergy-type reactions than any other substance on the average.

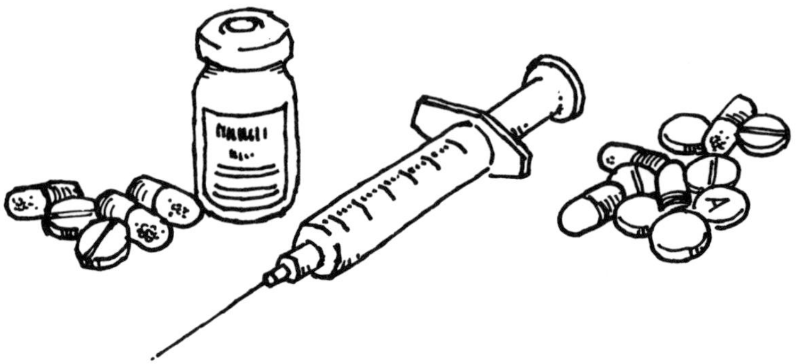

A. DMSO may increase or decrease the effect of the drugs.

The first and perhaps foremost precaution that should be taken by anyone using DMSO on themselves concerns the possible effect of DMSO on the action of other drugs. DMSO has been reported to multiply the effectiveness of some drugs and to suppress the activity of others. Reports on specific medications are poorly documented.

Persons using DMSO may find they can decrease their normal dosage of sleeping pills, tranquilizers, and possibly alcohol. The diabetic may find that the daily amount of insulin can be decreased. The diabetic can easily monitor the insulin present in the urine and make appropriate adjustments.

The best policy is simply to be aware of the possible connection between the use of DMSO and the possible effects on other medications taken during the same period. Whenever making such evaluations, ask the opinion of others. Self-diagnosis can be biased by the effect or concern about the effect itself. Preferably, with any but the most familiar medications you should ask your physician to help you monitor changes and decide on appropriate adjustments.

In some cases it may be best to avoid using DMSO while taking other drugs. For instance, although no conclusive evidence of any liver damage has ever been reported, a few cases of abnormalities in liver function tests have been noted. Anyone with known liver disease or taking drugs known to have toxic side effects involving the liver should exercise extra caution when using DMSO. If you don't know whether a drug you are taking has occasional toxic

effects on the liver - find out. Ask you physician or your pharmacist. It may be possible to have your physician monitor your liver function during any DMSO therapy if any question still remains.

B. DMSO may serve as a vehicle to carry other - possibly undesirable - substances through the skin into the blood.

DMSO is an excellent solvent, and the number of possible contaminants is as large as the number of substances that might be dissolved in it. One should take care to assure that the supply of DMSO is uncontaminated. Keep and use it in a way that will avoid any contamination.

As a firm rule, keep any DMSO used for garden, pet or household solvent purposes completely separate from any DMSO intended for human use.

A sensible precaution is to cleanse the skin before topical application. But there is no reason to be obsessed or excessive about this. The dangers on any given occasion are largely a matter of the poisons one may have been in contact with. There is no danger from perspiration or natural skin secretions. Furthermore, unless you have been dealing with something particularly deadly, it is unlikely that anything carried into the skin with DMSO will cause tremendous harm. The general precaution of cleansing the area of application as a rule takes into consideration that you may be exposed to toxic substances without being aware of it.

C. DMSO should not be administered in women known to be pregnant, or in breast-feeding mothers.

The amount of data available on the actions of DMSO during pregnancy are insufficient to be 100% sure of its safety.

Recently, after many years of common use, both caffeine and small amounts of alcohol (one drink per day), have been shown to increase the rate of birth defects. DMSO has not been tested in sufficient detail to be able to say that it is safer than these other more common substances.

The greatest temptation for the pregnant mother appears to be to use DMSO to alleviate lower back pain during pregnancy. Such a use **cannot possibly be justified** on the basis of current knowledge. There is an unacceptable risk.

In women of child-bearing age, it is, of course, possible you might inadvertently use DMSO during an early stage, before you know you are pregnant. There is no specific data that is grounds for expecting a problem. However, there is an unknown risk factor. If you are contemplating a planned pregnancy, avoid use of DMSO. There is an unacceptable risk.

Avoid the use of DMSO while breast-feeding. Again, there is insufficient data to establish safety during this delicate period of infant development.

Side Effects and How to Deal with Them

The two most important common reported side effects of DMSO therapies are the breath odor and the temporary skin reactions. Except for regular users, the breath problem is nothing but a nuisance. It has been characterized as similar to "oyster-breath," "garlic-breath," clam-breath," and humorlessly by young athletes as "death-breath." The DMSO breath-odor is sufficiently distinctive that once you have been around it you can almost always recognize it. DMSO users form a sort of underground community. It is often the excuse for starting a conversation with a stranger, and has probably been the stimulus to more than one friendship.

Dealing with the Breath Odor

Nothing seems to mask the breath-odor, although breath mints (preferably Wintergreen), mouth wash and so forth help a little. Perfumes help but don't really solve the problem.

The odor is usually attributed to DMS. In fact, we know that DMS is part of the smell of fresh seafood. However, anyone who has smelled pure DMS knows that it cannot account fully for the breath-odor. Pure DMS has an ether-like smell that is not really particularly unpleasant. Something in DMSO-breath is really, although only mildly, off-putting.

The best hypothesis is that some substance from the mercaptan family is produced when the body processes DMSO. Mercaptans in extremely small quantities - really just a few molecules - are notoriously bad smelling. Interestingly, only 80%-90% of DMSO users notice the odor; however, others notice it on the breath of those users who don't notice it on themselves. There is no real understanding of this at the moment.

The Skin Reaction: Evaluation and Response

The skin reaction has two aspects - an itch and a superficial inflammation. In severe cases, the itch becomes a serious discomfort, and the inflammation develops into something very much like a sunburn, complete with numerous tiny blisters. This is to be distinguished from a generalized urticaria or hives that has been reported to occur in rare instances.

Those persons with light-colored skin or with normally sensitive skin should expect some skin reaction. Curiously, it may not happen on the first or first few applications - it can apparently happen at any time. (This is not surprising to those who frequently experience rashes of unknown origin.)

The skin reaction typically occurs within a couple of minutes if it is going to happen, and most of the DMSO has not penetrated and can be washed off. Cold water is adequate, and will serve to cool the skin as well. The discomfort and rash may continue for some time. The rash is usually treated like a sunburn. All standard treatments for sunburn have been used successfully in treating the DMSO skin rash. Some remnants of the rash may persist for a couple of weeks. Simple skin loss, as with sunburn, has been reported in a few cases.

Those experiencing a severe skin rash may decide that this side effect is more troubling than the original problem to be treated. There are alternative treatments for almost every medical condition where DMSO has shown benefit.

When there is a mild itching and rash, this is typically reported to lessen with repeated daily applications to the same area. The explanation that has been suggested is that the cells have used up all their histamine. The skin reaction is thought to result from a histamine release. This is a standard response to an irritant. However, with DMSO, it may be that the histamine release is caused by an alteration to the cell structure, not indicating a real irritation reaction to the DMSO. The skin rash is self-limiting - meaning that although unpleasant, it will gradually get better by itself.

INVESTIGATOR'S EVALUATION OF OVERALL THERAPEUTIC RESULT

Therapeutic Result		Percent of Total Patients	
		Acute	Chronic
Excellent		46.4	24.2
Good		26.0	27.6
Fair		12.2	16.0
Poor		14.9	31.7
Blank*		0.5	0.5
	Total	100.0	100.0
	Total Patients	1,068	848

*Evaluation not supplied by investigator.

Demos *et al.*: *DMSO in Muskeloskeletal Disorders* (141:521)

The best clinical investigation of other side effects of topical DMSO comes from the toxicity studies on prisoners at the State Prison Hospital at Vacaville, California. In both the 14 day and 90 day studies, the prisoners applied large amounts of DMSO daily in a gel form to their skin. Keeping in mind these were large doses, the DMSO-linked side effects other than the expected breath odor and skin reaction, included:

14-Day Study
Sedation
Headache
Nausea
Dizziness

90-Day Study
Sedation
Occasional insomnia
Nausea
Dizziness
Diarrhea

There is no doubt that these side effects were due to DMSO. However, it is not clear whether they are likely to occur with normal clinical doses.

When high concentrations of DMSO are used, there does appear to be a fairly unique group of responses that might be classified together as "the third side effect." It includes a peculiar sort of headache, a mild tranquilizer-type effect, and a faint sort of dizziness. When the dizziness is pronounced, one sometimes feels a little nausea.

Limited reports suggest that neither aspirin nor Tylenol help the headache. The headache (a "DMSO headache") is more like a discomfort, like something one might associate with a head cold or mild sinus pressure. The headache may last all day, but apparently disappears with a night's sleep. It is not very intense and does not require cessation of most activities.

This "third side effect" seems to be sporadic like the mild skin reaction. It doesn't seem to occur regularly. Since it is so mild under normal clinical conditions, most reports are vague and anecdotal. If it hadn't been for the Vacaville studies, it is unlikely that clinicians could have identified it at all.

SIDE EFFECTS OF TOPICALLY APPLIED DMSO IN 4180 PATIENTS

John and Laudahn: *Clinical Experiences of DMSO* (141:515)

Local dermatitis	3.5%
Generalized dermatitis	0.1%
Nausea, headache	1.6%
Changes of eyesight	no reports, no clinical evidence

To remove a large dose (say 8 ounces or more) taken by mouth, induce vomiting and proceed to an emergency room to have as much as possible of the remaining dose removed by stomach pump (Labage).

All known benefits of DMSO occur at relatively low dosages, and all the discomforting side effects increase with dosage and concentration. Consequently, there is no advantage, and many disadvantages, in taking large doses of DMSO. In any case, an accidental, lethal overdose with DMSO is almost impossible. In fact, a lethal overdose would be difficult to achieve by some routes, even if you worked at it. As a rough measure, the dangers of overdosing with DMSO are roughly the same - in terms of quantity - as with alcohol. However, the actual effects would be unique to DMSO. (You don't get drunk, for instance.)

Using a 90% DMSO gel, you would need to use at least a quart (32 ounces) - possibly two or more, for an average sized adult. Assuming two ounces covers the body, and a minimum of 60 minutes between topical applications to allow for complete absorption, it would take 16 hours or more to approach a lethal dose. Since about half the DMSO is metabolized in 6 hours, it is likely that in humans you would need to continue application for several days to reach a lethal dose.

Another way to represent this is to say that if you filled a bathtub with 90% DMSO and immersed yourself in it, you would probably have to wait at least 16 to 24 hours for a lethal effect. Animal experiments using rats and mice immersed up to their necks in 100% DMSO showed that "most died within 24 hours." But only "some" died when the concentration was 80% DMSO (for 24 hours). Since the amount of surface area, where DMSO can enter, is much greater per body volume in the smaller animals, it is likely that the lethal dose for humans is even more difficult to achieve by this procedure.

Drinking DMSO, you could conceivably achieve a lethal effect with about a quart and a half of 80% DMSO. Vomiting is likely to occur long before this much could be downed. With a small child, drinking a full pint (8 ounces) directly could prove lethal. But again, vomiting is likely to remove much of the dose. Induce vomiting, if possible, to remove such a dose, and proceed to an emergency room to have the stomach pumped out (Labage).

With large non-lethal doses, an intense sulfate odor on the exhaled breath is noticed, and there is an apparent sedation, with decreased motor activity. For further details refer to the discussions of the Vacaville studies in the **Toxicity** and **Side Effects Section**.

4

HOW TO USE DMSO

General Considerations

First Principle. There is one foremost principle to keep in mind in the use of DMSO for medical conditions: DMSO is best considered a **supportive therapy** rather than as a substitute or replacement for conventional treatments.

Even before actual treatment, for those deciding to self-medicate, the greatest errors have always been in the diagnosis stage. Because of the way our personalities are tied up with our injuries or illnesses, self-diagnosis is a foolish practice. Lack of knowledge and experience also usually mean that the non-professional is less likely to be able to distinguish one type of injury or illness from another.

Furthermore, when one is really uncertain about the diagnosis, it is extremely difficult to monitor the progress of the condition or benefits of the course of treatment. For many people who tell you how DMSO did or did not work, applied in one way or another for a particular condition, the real truth is often likely to be that they were not treating the condition they thought they were. This problem arises enough with trained physicians to make one suspect that in general 1/3 to 1/2 (perhaps more) of all non-professional diagnoses are mistaken to some significant extent - the message here should be clear, but let it be stated explicitly.

If you think you have a condition serious enough to treat with DMSO, it is likely that it is serious enough to deserve both diagnosis and monitoring by a trained professional.

If you do decide to monitor your own progress and treatment with DMSO, keep a record of (a) what you think you are treating; (b) when you started treatment; and (c) how the symptoms have behaved. Many physicians will work with patients interested in trying DMSO. Anyone contemplating a self-medication program with DMSO should at least telephone their physician for advice on other additional therapies and how they do or do not combine with DMSO. Also, it is wise to keep your physician informed of any developments - bad or good, and ask for help in interpreting them properly.

Interaction with Other Therapies

Returning to our **first principle**, that DMSO is a supportive therapy, an important question must be how DMSO harmonizes with other therapies and other medications. The answer, unfortunately, for most conditions, is that we simply don't know. The majority of clinical research on arthritis, sports injuries and pain, undertaken since the early 1960's, remains unpublished. Some facts are known, and a few can be reasoned. However, **due to the general lack of knowledge, the only sensible policy is not to mix therapies, or when doing so, be alert to any possible interactions**. Anyone taking other medications or involved in any other therapies for other conditions, should definitely consult their physician before trying DMSO.

Consult the index and review the Questions Section for further information. If in doubt about a combination, don't.

Interaction with Other Drugs

DMSO enhances the effectiveness of some drugs, and reduces the effectiveness of others. All drugs appear to gain a better distribution with DMSO, and it is hypothesized that this may account for many of the observed enhancement effects.

Originally it was noticed that persons using tranquilizers, sleeping pills and pain relieving medication found these medications to have increased potency. They found the same relief could be obtained with lesser dosages of the original medication. However, since it is now known that DMSO produces a sedative effect by itself, no one is completely clear as to whether the effects are additive or whether DMSO is really amplifying the original drugs. It seems likely that both are occurring, but there are no published research findings.

What is Best: Liquid, Lotion or Gel

DMSO is now appearing on the People's Market in lotion and gel forms, in addition to the standard liquid form. Needless to say, there is something added to the lotion and gel forms as thickening agents. The two agents most commonly used - as far as can be easily determined - seem to be hydroxyethylcellulose and carboxyethylcellulose. The large European pharmaceutical corporation Schering A.G. (Berlin), reported using hydroxyethylcellulose "as a thickening agent to facilitate application" of a 90% DMSO solution. The report covers therapeutic trials on 4,180 patients during the summer of 1964. No toxicity or side effects from the topical applications were reported that could be distinguished from those expected with DMSO.

These two thickening agents are very common in other lotion medications and cosmetics. They are generally considered to be very safe for external

application. However, there are no published reports of experiments to determine if DMSO reacts with either of these - or any other - thickening agents to produce secondary products.

It is certainly conceivable that there is a reaction, and that some of the minor secondary products are toxic. Published results (and substantial private reports), indicate there is no immediately noticeable acute toxicity. However, there may well be some long term toxicity. Stated simply - we just don't know. But finally, it must be added that talking about "potential dangers" in an area of ignorance is difficult, and it is even more difficult to decide what to conclude as far as practical action is concerned.

There is no published evidence on whether DMSO carries these thickening agents through the skin into the blood. Considering the size of the mole- cules, one would expect some penetration. Background evidence on these agents indicates that they are probably not dangerous taken internally in small amounts, and are easily expelled by the body.

The use of DMSO in a lotion or gel slows down the rate of absorption and penetration of the DMSO into the skin. The best estimates available suggest a doubling of the time for a dose of DMSO to penetrate fully. For some people, this slow-down has been an advantage. A high concentration - for instance 90% rather than 70% - can be used without experiencing skin irritation.

Some people may find less skin irritation with a lotion or gel. But the same relief can perhaps be gained by reducing the concentration of DMSO. In short, the only real advantage of the lotion or gel is convenience. Liquid DMSO is difficult to apply because drops form and run down your arm or leg, or whatever.

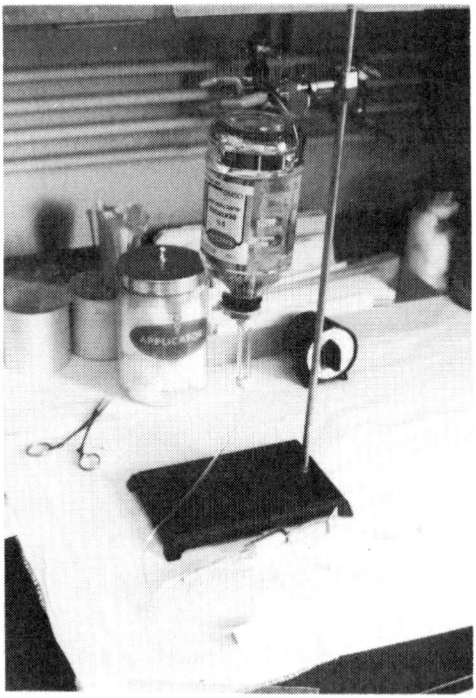

Route of Administration

Without the aide of a physician, there are only two reasonable routes of administration for DMSO: topically and orally. The toxicity studies in animals have evaluated both these routes without finding any significant difference. However, there have been no formally controlled human studies.

Limitations on Oral Administration

In a series of informal human studies, it was found that oral DMSO decreases the output of digestive acid in the stomach. As a consequence, food does not digest as easily or completely as it should, resulting in gas and indigestion. The physicians involved concluded that there were no advantages to oral administration of DMSO, other than convenience, and some additional inconvenient side effects. They no longer prescribe DMSO orally for their patients, except in unusual circumstances.

Some persons who were part of these early (unpublished) clinical trials on oral DMSO prefer this route, and continue to take DMSO orally. Usually, one or two teaspoons of DMSO in fruit juice (grape is the favorite) is taken at bedtime. Avoiding periods four hours or more before or after a mealtime may lessen the digestive interference.

Even for people with generalized conditions, like whole-body (poly-) arthritis, the topical route of administration appears to be preferable. DMSO has a systemic as well as a local effect. Once it enters the body, it is circulated throughout and acts on the whole-body chemistry. There is some additional benefit to the local site of application, but for a generalized condition this is less important. In treating a generalized condition, simply select a couple of the most troublesome areas and apply as you would normally.

Topical Application Procedures

In applying DMSO topically, avoid the most sensitive skin areas - the neck, groin, and behind the knee. Here, the skin is thin and any irritation that may occur would be more troublesome.

Application should be over a large area to help in absorption. The greater the area covered by a certain amount of DMSO, the shorter will be the time for absorption. If you limit application to a small area, the DMSO may have to be administered several times before it all soaks in. This takes a longer time.

We have prepared a chart to serve as a rough "rule of thumb" guide in the topical application of DMSO for common musculoskeletal conditions. Particular care should be taken in applying DMSO in the region of the head. All mucous surfaces are more susceptible to irritation and more troublesome when they do become irritated.

Other than these normal precautions, there is no particular danger when DMSO comes in contact with the eye. No one should consider applying DMSO to the eye as a treatment, unless under the direct supervision of an opthalmologist or physician.

Topical Application Chart — I

Cover a large area surrounding the joint or muscle as indicated: 1) elbow 2) knee 3) shoulder 4) wrist or hand 5) hip joint 6) ankle or foot.

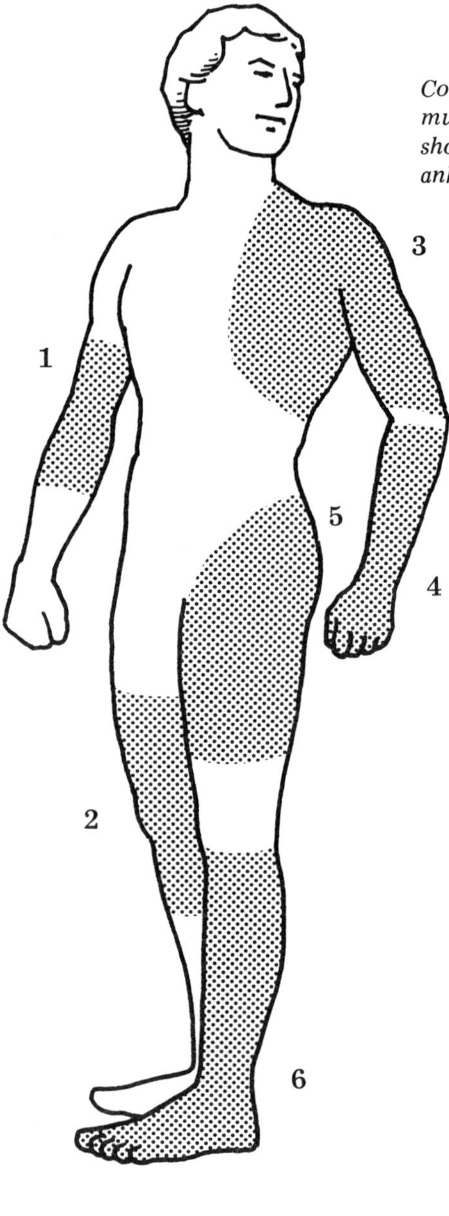

The Best Concentration

The concentration of DMSO used in several conditions appears to be important to the results. In other words, three applications of 30% DMSO do not produce the same biological effects as one application of 90% DMSO, even though the total amount of DMSO may be the same. This sort of "dose-dependency" is common with most therapeutic agents.

There are no controlled studies on DMSO to prove this or to clarify the exact proper concentrations for best results. With DMSO, the local effect on wounds or injuries of muscles and associated structures is most dependent on concentration. The general systemic effects can be brought about with several applications of lesser concentration. None of this is particularly surprising.

For most conditions calling for local, topical application, the best concentration is anything greater than 67% and yet less than 90% DMSO.

Harmony of 67% DMSO

The reason for the lower limit of 67% (or really .66666...equals 2/3) traces back to the fact when DMSO is mixed with water it forms a **hydrate** - a loose complex of two molecules of DMSO with each molecule of water. The hydrate complex cannot really be classified as a new molecular compound, because the three parts are not bound tightly enough.

When more water is added, the DMSO still remains in this two-to-one hydrate complex. Concentrations less than 67% take longer to penetrate the skin and enter the body. This is apparently due to a balancing of the attraction of the water in the body and on the skin. But this is speculative, since the precise mechanism of penetration is not understood.

90% DMSO is First Choice

One of the most curious observations concerning the mechanism of penetration of DMSO through biological membranes is that 100% penetrates **more slowly** than 90%. The 90% DMSO concentration is the fastest penetrating. This has lead to speculation that the real explanation will require a better understanding of the electrostatic structure and processes of membranes. DMSO is well-known as a substance that can significantly alter electrostatic patterns of solutions. This is part of the secret of its usefulness in the chemical industry.

For those who can apply 90% DMSO without any skin irritation, it is the concentration of choice, largely because it takes only five-ten minutes to absorb (as evidenced by dryness on the skin surface). From this concentration to all lower concentrations, the more water in the DMSO solution, the longer it takes to absorb. (For those who might apply 100% DMSO without a skin reaction, there is a "dimpling" of the flesh indicating a slight dehydration of the tissues. This is temporary and disappears in one - three hours.)

When applying DMSO to mucous membranes - any of the body's naturally moist surfaces - the concentration should be 50% or less. The concentration of DMSO in injections given by physicians has typically been 20% DMSO.

Intravenous DMSO has been given at concentrations as high as 40% DMSO. However, this causes massive breakdown of red blood cells - presumably because of the high concentration gradient at the point of entry into the blood. Curiously, people receiving these highly concentrated intravenous infusions have not suffered the normally expected toxic side effects of red blood cell breakdown. DMSO itself appears to protect the patient from the damage that is caused by these high concentration infusions.

The most recent experiments have shown that intravenous infusions of 10% DMSO in cases of severe head trauma produce the same benefits as 40% and 20% DMSO - without the worrisome side effect of red blood cell breakdown.

Dosage and Time

This section is designed to introduce the reader to what is known, in answer to the following commonly asked questions, about the application of DMSO:

1. When to apply it?
2. How much to apply?
3. How often?
4. How long to continue?

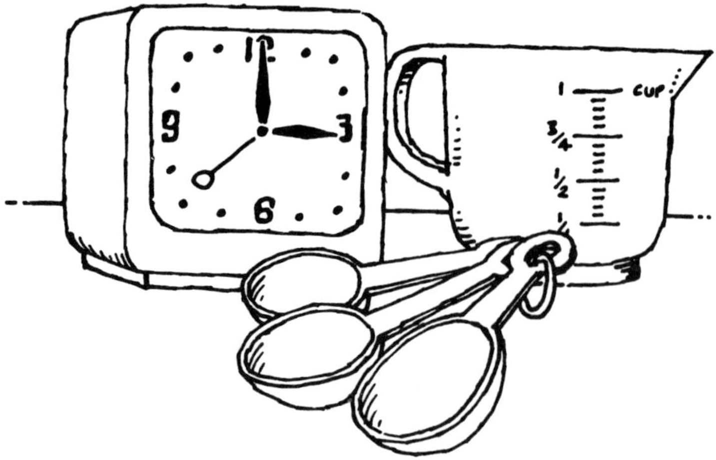

When to Apply DMSO?

Very generally speaking, there is no reason to prefer taking DMSO at one time of day rather than another. Morning, afternoon and evening are all equally acceptable.

When applying DMSO topically, there is no effect one way or another in relation to mealtime. If oral DMSO is necessary, avoid a broad period several hours before and after meals or snacks.

Avoid the periods one hour before and one hour after bath, shower or swimming. If applied before, the DMSO may wash out of the skin. If applied after, it is diluted by the large amount of water captured in the skin.

How Much to Apply?

The normal dosage of each application is 5 - 15 milliliters, or equivalently 1 - 3 teaspoons of 70% - 90% DMSO. More specifically and technically, the clinical dose of each application is usually about 10 - 20 milligrams of DMSO per kilogram of body weight of the patient; 0.1 - 0.2g/kg, b.w. The total dosage received during treatment is then determined by how often these standard applications take place and how long they continue.

How Often?

Successful application has been reported at frequencies ranging from hourly to once or twice a week for some of the same conditions. Many of the questions about dosage, frequency and duration of treatment remain largely open.

Physical therapists and athletic team trainers have often recommended applications every 1 - 2 hours immediately after an injury for the first half-day or evening. Every 4 hours the second day is common. These cases of extreme frequency only make sense in acute injuries where it is imperative to control swelling and keep healing processes operative. A similar approach has been reported in the successful treatment of bruises such as "black eyes" during the first one to two days.

By the second or third day, applications every 4 - 6 hours seem to be sufficient for maximum benefit, although there are some exceptions.

For conditions dominated by pain and for inflammation, the general rule seems to be once every 4 - 6 hours, as needed. Some need greater frequency regularly, and some only occasionally. Others find once or twice a week gives the same benefits (see the discussion of **Interval Therapy**).

How Long to Continue?

The length of treatment depends heavily on the type of condition. In acute musculoskeletal injuries, most benefits are obtained within five days of treatment. One additional application on the 7th - 10th day may be worthwhile.

Chronic conditions require much longer than acute conditions. Treatment of acute conditions is normally completed in 5 - 7 days with a few taking up to three weeks, and the rare exception longer. Chronic conditions may not even show significant benefit until 6 - 8 weeks after treatment has begun. Continuing improvement of benefits experienced with each week of applications have been reported commonly, up to 3 - 6 months. Relief in long established conditions is usually only partial, even in the long-run. But dramatic reversals of debilitating conditions that have lasted for months and years is not at all uncommon with DMSO.

This broad range of treatment periods and response time, and the fact that some receive almost immediate major relief while others experience slow, gradual benefit, only after weeks of conscientious treatment, has undoubtedly fueled the controversy about DMSO. But the facts are facts. The experienced clinician will not be surprised by this range of response with DMSO. Many other therapeutic agents have equally broad response characteristics. The explanation is usually traceable to underlying major differences in superficially similar conditions.

Preliminary Self-test

Testing Yourself for Sensitivity

Other than the apparently unavoidable breath odor, the next most common side effect of topical DMSO is the mild skin reaction. The skin reaction is the best single sign of whether you are likely to have an unacceptable level of the minor side effects with DMSO. Some people experience a more severe rash with fine little sunburn-like blisters. If you are someone with normally sensitive skin, if you easily sunburn, and mild rashes are fairly common, it is likely that you will experience a significant skin reaction with DMSO. Some people find this problem serious enough to discontinue all use of DMSO.

Before using DMSO for any actual ailment, it is wise to test yourself for sensitivity to skin reaction. If you know you have sensitive skin, start by diluting your DMSO down to 25% DMSO/75% water. Apply a few drops to the back of your hand and spread it around a little. Let it soak in for 15 minutes, unless you begin to notice a significant reddening or flush. If a rash begins to appear, just rinse the remaining DMSO off your hand. If the discomfort and rash persist, try soaking for a few minutes in cold water, then apply any standard hand cream (for instance, Vaseline Intensive Care, etc.). Like a sunburn or other rash, it might be gone in a few hours, perhaps a couple of days, or it might gradually disappear over two weeks.

It is normal to experience some discomfort - an itch like you want to scratch the area. Don't. But if you experience serious discomfort at this level, it is likely you are too skin sensitive to use DMSO. It is possible to give yourself a pretty serious burn with DMSO. But this is much less likely if you take these precautions and test yourself for sensitivity first.

Evaluating Your Response to DMSO

Basic judgment is needed making evaluations. If what happens at 25% DMSO doesn't bother you, you are cleared to check out 50%. If you are not normally skin sensitive, you might start at 50%. If you are comfortable with 50%, then you might try 70%. If at some point you are considering using 90%, wait until you have more experience with 70%. All the minor side effects increase with increased concentration.

The skin rash is not an all or nothing question. You are the one that must decide whether you are willing to put up with the degree of reaction (if any) that you experience. Some people don't notice any rash until the third or fourth day of treatment. The skin rash is about as serious as a sunburn - although you could probably make things worse if you really work at it. If you experience a rash that is worse than a sunburn, or have any other questions, don't hesitate to contact your physician.

Clinical reports indicate that if you continue to apply DMSO at a moderate 50% to 70% concentration while experiencing mild skin rash, the rash will tend to decrease over time. This is the opposite of what happens with allergic reactions. The rash is felt to be the result of a histamine release. If you continue to apply DMSO, with discretion, the histamine reserves in that area of skin become depleted and the rash fades.

If you are faced with a situation where you have a mild skin rash, but gain relief for another condition - ask for advice. Ask your physician to help you decide whether the benefits are worth the side effects. Ask a friend. Don't rely on your evaluation alone.

Many more people experience an occasional temporary rash rather than the regular and persistent rash. When you notice a rash, you might stop using DMSO temporarily, or cut down the strength, and don't hesitate to treat the rash with the skin cream or lotion.

The skin reaction occurs only at the site of application. If you experience a rash elsewhere, it is most probably for another reason. A rare possibility is a mild allergic reaction resulting in hives - see below.

Different Responses in Acute and Chronic Conditions

All health problems can be generally separated into those that are acute and those that are chronic. **Acute disorders** are usually single, non-recurring flare-ups. **Chronic disorders** are either constantly troublesome over an indefinite period, or display a pattern of repeated discomfort, suggesting an ongoing underlying disease process.

Virtually all researchers in the several major clinical studies of DMSO report a significant difference generally in response with acute versus chronic conditions. One researcher discussed his results as follows: "DMSO was employed as a topical agent in 500 different cases in a variety of clinical disorders. These constituted mainly acute and chronic musculoskeletal diseases. The chronic disorders required continued application of the drug in order to control the symptoms. The more acute conditions would often completely subside without further occurrence. The chronic disease states would frequently relapse on the withdrawal of the drug." "In general, the greater the chronicity of the disorder, the longer the treatment with DMSO must be employed in order to achieve palliation. In these instances, DMSO is not a cure, but does afford symptomatic relief." (141:548).

Another researcher makes the same point very concisely: "It is difficult to declare that a drug has efficacy on the basis of uncontrolled studies in a heterogeneous group of diseases. However, from these data and from discussions with many of our investigators, we feel that DMSO is a unique and effective agent for the treatment of many acute musculoskeletal disorders. Beneficial results are unpredictable, but they occur frequently and are sometimes dramatic, particularly in acute conditions, which require low doses and short treatment periods. In chronic conditions, improvement occurs at a lower rate and is less dramatic."

A researcher dealing exclusively with genitourinary disorders was struck by the fact that "although many fail to benefit in any way whatsoever, there were some who obtained dramatic and gratifying relief of symptoms."

In general, the onset of the beneficial effect clearly occurred earlier in acute cases than in chronic ones, and the effect itself was of longer duration as well.

Since many of those reading this book are completely unfamiliar with test results on other drugs, they may find it difficult to interpret some of these comments. First, it is almost always true that a fair percentage of people (5%-50%) are not helped by even the best of medications. There is almost never a known explanation for this.

With DMSO, as with other medications and treatments, there are hypotheses about why two cases that **look** identical don't respond the same. However, more and more physicians are beginning to use the failure to respond to DMSO therapy as an important observation suggesting a need to

COMPARATIVE EVALUATION OF THE EFFECT OF DMSO IN ACUTE AND CHRONIC MUSCULOSKELETAL DISORDERS

	No. of Cases	Partial Remission of Symptoms	Complete Remission of Symptoms	Failures
Acute disorders	1025	279 = 27.2%	609 = 59.4%	137 = 13.4%
Chronic disorders	3155	1088 = 34.5%	1572 = 49.8%	495 = 15.7%
Total	4180			

John and Laudahn: *Clinical Experiences of DMSO* (141:509)

revise the diagnosis. One researcher stated: "The therapeutic specificity of DMSO in post-traumatic soft tissue injuries is such that, in my opinion, failure of benefit within 24 hours after DMSO application may postulate toward error in initial diagnosis, or toward psychosomatic influences causing persistence of symptoms."

General Remarks About Dosage and Response

Most acute severe injuries are well under control within 24 hours of initiation of DMSO treatment. The treatment schedule usually involves application of DMSO every four to six hours to begin with, and only as much as necessary to relieve pain and assure mobility thereafter. The overall duration of treatment time varies with the type of condition and extent of injury.

Several published reports indicate that athletic team physicians have tried applying DMSO topically every two hours during the first 24 hours. This has apparently been successful in relieving pain and particularly, swelling. But there are no comparative studies that would allow us to conclude that the two hour scheduling is better than the four-six intervals. If anything, the more likely hypothesis is that even less frequently would obtain the same results. Control of pain is a good indication of whether another application is appropriate.

As a rule of thumb, three applications the first day, two applications on the second, and a final application on the fourth or fifth day should complete the treatment of acute musculoskeletal problems.

In a large sampling, treatment of most acute conditions was completed in less than eight days with only a small percentage finding treatment desirable up to 35 days. Only in exceptional cases did treatment continue for up to six weeks.

Each topical application of DMSO is assumed to be from 5-15 milliliters applied over a large area including the site of the problem. According to the American Standards Society, the teaspoon in the American household is about 5 milliliters. So each application is one-to-three teaspoons of 70%-90% DMSO.

In one published study with over 1,000 patients, in a mixed sampling of acute and chronic disorders, the overall average daily dose per person was calculated to be between 7-14 milliliters - roughly one to three teaspoons per person per day. Fifty-five percent of the acute patients used less than 60 milliliters (12 teaspoons) total during the entire course of treatment. As a comparison, 42 percent of the chronics used less than 60 milliliters (during the treatment period of "up to 21 days"). Fourteen percent of the acute patients and 30 percent of the chronic patients used more than 200 milliliters. Twelve percent of the chronic patients used more than 500 milliliters (all of these exceeding the 21 day treatment period). In general, the lower dosage in the acute group was related directly to the shorter treatment period.

Chronic disorders in general required longer treatment to obtain a significant effect and for maximum effect. Some relief is usually realized immediately or within the first week. Average treatment period for an episode ranges from three-six weeks.

The Carryover

More than one researcher has noticed that once relief has been obtained in a chronic condition (the major symptom is usually pain), and DMSO treatments are stopped, there is no recurrence for a period of from five days to five weeks. This has been referred to as "the carryover period," when the beneficial effects of the early DMSO treatment carry over into the non-treatment period.

There is an interesting story associated with these findings. No physician would normally ask his patient to cease a successful treatment for a chronic condition to wait for a full recurrence (relapse), just to see how long it would take. The first observation of a carryover effect arose when the FDA in November, 1965, called a halt to all human clinical studies of DMSO. Several thousand patients had been receiving DMSO during 1965. Many chronic pain sufferers who had gained relief from DMSO where all else had failed turn out to be unwilling subjects in a rather brutal experiment - to see how long before their former painful condition returned. There was, in fact, some surprise that it took as long as it did, and this became one of the motivations for the investigations of Dr. Marvin Paul in what he terms "interval therapy."

Note: Most clinicians (and particularly DMSO supporters) took this "accidental" experiment to be another experimental control - as good as or better than a double-blind experiment. But the FDA rejected this data as unscientific. Only **their** double-blind design qualifies something to be scientific.

Interval Therapy

Dr. Marvin Paul of Toronto, Canada (at one time the team physician of the Toronto Mapleleafs) in association with Merck, Sharp and Dohme, of Canada Limited, investigated the possibility of using DMSO much less frequently than had become - and still is - the general practice. Following the initial reports of its potential use as a pharmacologic agent, most investigators applied DMSO from two to four times daily.

In Dr. Paul's study, 180 patients were treated once or twice a week with DMSO, two teaspoons 80% DMSO per treatment. Among the categories of disease evaluated were acute injuries, chronic rheumatoid arthritis, cervical and lumbar disc syndrome, varicose veins, acute and chronic sinusitis, and thrombophlebitis.

According to Paul, the results achieved in this study compared favorably with those obtained by others administering the same dosage twice daily.

The Priming Effect

During the study mentioned above, Dr. Paul recorded a curious observation in a significant number of patients. "An individual showing little or no response to DMSO following the first application frequently exhibited a dramatic response four to seven days following the second application. This was particularly true in treating the patient with a chronic disability. This 'delayed-action' phenomenon may represent a 'priming effect.'" Forty-six of 180 patients, or 26 percent, treated with DMSO reacted in this way. Paul felt that the more chronic the condition, the more likely this was to occur.

The initial application of DMSO in these patients perhaps "primed" them for subsequent treatment with the drug without the initial treatment demonstrating any observed therapeutic significance. In his discussion, Paul notes that this "priming" phenomenon might not have been observed had the DMSO been given once or twice daily rather than once or twice weekly. Finally, he speculates that this effect may well take place with many of our modern therapeutic agents, but that the standardization of the daily dosage routine might be obscuring its observation.

Note: It is worth mentioning that the pharmaceutical industry, which funds virtually all drug research, would experience a considerable economic setback if Paul's general hypothesis about "priming" is ever confirmed. Homeopathic medicine, in its more rigorous scientific form, would argue that they have a great deal of evidence to support such a claim. However, until recently such phenomena were considered evidence of "psychological cures." With the advances of cybernetics and systems theory in medicine, the argument that the body might, in some instances, be able to make a "cooperative" or "intelligent" response to a medication or treatment is far more credible.

SPECIFIC APPLICATIONS — I

5

Arthritis

The Common Forms of Arthritis

Currently, there is no cure for arthritis. This includes DMSO. Not only is there no cure, but by and large, no one knows for sure what causes it.

The word "arthritis" literally means inflammation of a joint. Arthritis, however, is not a single disease, but a term to cover close to 100 conditions that cause aches and pains around joints and connective tissues. To make matters worse, medical professionals in different countries use significantly different terms and definitions to describe what they see in patients. In Great Britain, the term "rheumatism" is a vague word also used to describe unexplained aches and pains in joints and muscles. Rheumatism covers all forms of arthritis, but in the United States, it refers only to disease that **does not** involve joints.

There is a diversity of responses to specific treatment regimens that rivals the diversity of arthritis conditions themselves. What helps one person, often dramatically, does apparently nothing for others with what appear to be exactly the same symptoms. More often than not, the response is somewhere in between - some help. Many people report improvement from dietary changes or supplements. Others experience the steady progression of their disease despite all life-style changes and therapeutic changes.

Another quirk of arthritis is its high rate of spontaneous remission. Arthritis has a way of coming and going unpredictably. The pain and swelling can simply disappear for days, weeks or even months. Victims who experience such a remission are easily convinced that whatever they were taking or doing brought relief. But when we look at large numbers of people to test these hypotheses, nothing seems to check out. This includes the hypothesis that periods of suffering are brought on by emotional upsets. Nothing has checked out scientifically.

Hopefully, you are getting the impression that, so far at least, arthritis is somewhat of a medical enigma. If so, you won't be far off. However, there are some very specific differences among those reporting arthritic symptoms. In a small percentage of cases, there is a clear link to another disease process, the arthritis being a secondary consequence. And if the primary disease can be treated, the progression of the arthritic symptoms can be considerably slowed or stopped all together.

Among the more common broad categories - rheumatoid arthritis and osteoarthritis - there are definite, easily diagnosed differences. Because of the likelihood of having some of each, it is always best to have your physician perform the diagnostic tests. How best to proceed does depend on a proper diagnosis.

The most common forms of arthritis are rheumatoid arthritis, osteoarthritis, and gout.

Rheumatoid arthritis is the most serious because it is the most crippling of the three. It generally starts between the ages of 20 and 45, and affects three times as many women as men. Rheumatoid arthritis involves many joints, but most commonly the small joints of the hands. Inflammation and thickening of tissue around the joints may cause destruction of the bones, deformity and eventually disability. In some cases, the disease may be mild, in others it can be crippling. While the cause of rheumatoid arthritis is unknown, some scientists believe it may be sparked by a virus, while others feel the disease is linked to a disruption of the body's defense or immune system.

Osteoarthritis is often called the "wear and tear" disease. Chronic irritation of the joints, resulting from overweight, poor posture, injury or occupational strain, is a main factor in its development. Older people are the most frequent victims, and again, women are affected more often than men. The common symptoms of osteoarthritis are pain and stiffness. Pain is usually felt when certain joints are used, especially finger joints and those that bear the body's weight - namely knees, hips and spine. Disability most often occurs in these areas.

Gout is the easiest form of arthritis to diagnose and treat, and is the best understood. It most commonly affects the joints of the feet, particularly the big toe, although other joints may be involved. Nearly all cases of gout appear in men. Gout gets its start when too much of a certain body chemical, uric acid, is deposited in the tissues. Crystals of uric acid form in the joints, causing inflammation and severe pain. Attacks may follow minor injury, excessive eating or drinking, overexercise or surgery, or may occur for no apparent reason.

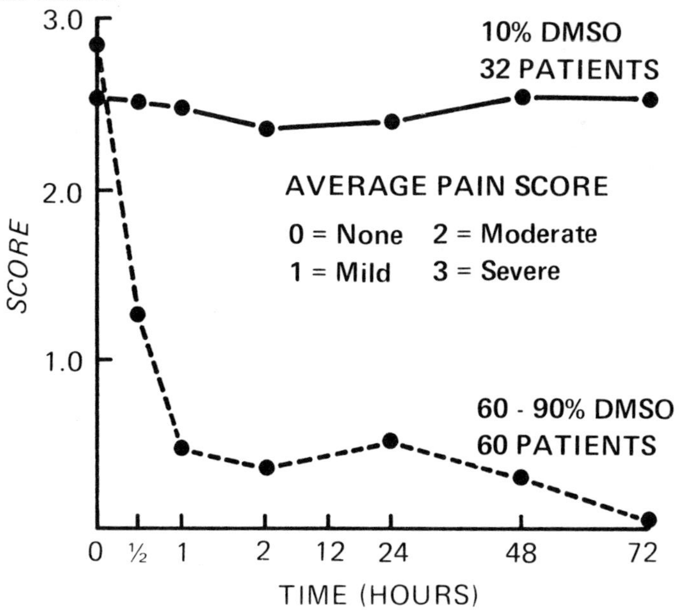

Comparison of effective DMSO solutions with placebo solution.

DMSO in Arthritis

DMSO was first tried in arthritis because of its already demonstrated activity as an anti-inflammatory and pain reliever.

Longer-term benefit from DMSO was also hoped for on the basis of evidence that showed that DMSO protects cells from damage and destruction in a variety of physically stressful situations.

As research has slowly progressed, several newer hypotheses have emerged to explain the reports of benefits with DMSO in arthritis. For instance, the striking ability of DMSO to scavenge free radicals - the most destructive chemicals in the body - has been shown to prevent breakdown of hyaluronic acid, the main lubricant for joints and tendons. Pain, at least over a period of days and weeks, may be relieved secondarily by maintaining adequate lubrication. And inflammation may be lessened, indirectly, by breaking the inflammatory cycle through the elmination of irritation in the joint. This occurs by DMSO helping to maintain adequate lubricant.

More Clues About Mechanism

DMSO is increasingly implicated in beneficial alterations of collagen metabolism and cellular proliferation. These processes are fundamental to several disease conditions associated with arthritis.

Collagen is the main protein of connective tissues. And as is natural, the region around joints contains a great deal of connective tissue. At certain stages in the development of rheumatoid arthritis and osteoarthritis, DMSO may have a beneficial effect in altering the abnormal collagen build-ups and destructive breakdowns.

In rheumatoid arthritis the earliest stages involve a cellular proliferation where certain tissues grow and infiltrate the joint abnormally. DMSO has been shown to alter abnormal cellular proliferation. If this is a cause of benefits, the **best** time to apply DMSO in rheumatoid arthritis is at the time of the **first flare-up**.

To decide conclusively whether this is likely to have a long-term effect in slowing the progress (or lessening the eventual severity) of rheumatoid arthritis would require a careful initial diagnosis and a long-term (ten to twenty years, at least) follow-up. But no one in the pharmaceutical industry or the government laboratories seems interested in pursuing these current clues.

DMSO has recently (**again**, really, since similar results were first noticed in 1975 and never followed up) been shown to have a significant effect in lowering the auto-immune antibodies. DMSO keeps getting positive results in auto-immune diseases. Rheumatoid arthritis has long been known to have a major auto-immune component. There have been inquiries about studies to

investigate this link but nothing has started. There are some basic researchers exploring the general link between DMSO and auto-immune antibodies.

DMSO In Rheumatoid Arthritis

DMSO appears to be less effective in rheumatoid arthritis than in osteoarthritis. The longer a person has had rheumatoid disease, the less likely he or she is to experience truly significant relief from DMSO. "In the acutely involved joint, the relief was prompt, but it was never complete." Successful treatment took longer in chronic sufferers who did, nonetheless, report significant benefits. The less involved the disease process, the greater the benefit from DMSO.

It is difficult to generalize the results, because some researchers reported a good-to-excellent response in **all** their rheumatoid arthritis patients. Other large studies indicate 50% good-to-excellent and 50% fair-to- poor response. Some of these differences were clearly due to differences in length of treatment. An excellent study by the Japanese Rheumatism Association concluded: "DMSO relieved joint pain, and increased the range of joint motion and grip strength, but the effect on decreasing joint swelling and local heat was not proved in this study (141:568)." They also noted a better response in the earlier stages of the disease process.

In some patients with extensive rheumatoid involvement, the DMSO was used as a supportive therapy, and enabled the patients to be carried on a smaller maintenance dose of Corticoid (141:536).

Dosage and Application: For acute attacks of arthritic pain and inflammation each treatment is one to three teaspoons (5-10 milliliters) of 70%-90% DMSO. This is applied topically to the skin over a large area surrounding the involved joint(s); see the Application Chart.

The typical frequency is once every 4-6 hours (or 2-4 times daily) in severe attacks. However, many find once daily or twice weekly adequate to obtain relief. A few people have reported significant improvement with applications every two hours for brief periods.

The only general rule is to **use as needed** in the judgment of the patient to obtain relief.

Once relief is obtained or has peaked, the patient should immediately attempt to reduce usage to discover the minimum dose needed to maintain relief. Maintenance can often be achieved with one treatment now and then - much less frequently.

Chronic sufferers start with two treatments daily, or more if results justify, for five days each week. (Some extreme cases may choose to treat seven days a week in the beginning.) It is necessary to maintain this program for 6-8 weeks before making conclusive evaluations of results. As Dr. Stanley W. Jacob often tells his patients: "DMSO is a slow worker. Don't get discouraged too soon." This is important to emphasize since many have come to expect an immediate response from misleading newspaper reports.

Once maximum relief is obtained, the chronic sufferer and user should seek to discover the minimum dose for maximum relief. Read the section on Interval Therapy.

As you may gather from the complications here, it is best to consult with your physician and have him/her supervise and monitor any DMSO therapy for arthritis. Otherwise, you may just end up playing around and not really knowing whether it is, or could be, of benefit to you in the long or short run.

Topical application is the preferred means of administrating DMSO for arthritis. There is no advantage to oral administration. Application should be to a large, clean area to help the speed of absorption. Wait 15-30 minutes for absorption and wipe off any remaining moisture.

Response: Pain relief and increased range of joint movement should occur in ten minutes to one hour, and last approximately 4-6 hours.

Long-term benefits in chronic sufferers are usually realized very gradually over a period of 6-8 weeks or longer. There are a number of reports of patients receiving increased benefits with each treatment for up to nine months. The degree of benefits in chronic cases usually reaches a maximum in 2-3 months.

Complete relief is only rarely obtained with DMSO alone.

The dramatic, rapid (1-2 day) relief experienced by some supposed arthritis patients (5%-10%) strongly suggests that the underlying cause of their condition was associated with some sort of bursitis-like deposit.

Special Precautions: Chronic patients electing to use DMSO over long periods should consider adopting the "five days on, two days off" program, with an occasional two-four week break every six months, to allow the body to eliminate the DMSO and to make any needed adjustments the DMSO might be preventing.

Be particularly careful when using DMSO long-term in conjunction with other medication. Consult your physician or pharmacist for advice.

DMSO in Osteoarthritis

The research results clearly demonstrate that DMSO is effective in alleviating both the immediate and long-term symptoms of osteoarthritis. Upwards of 84 percent of those participating in the major studies reported good-to- excellent therapeutic response.

These were not double-blind studies; however, as one researcher remarks: "Because of the chronic nature of this disorder, all of the patients had previously been treated by other modalities and hence serve as their own controls. Thus, in a given individual, a clinical pattern of symptomatology has been established prior to the use of DMSO. (141:533)."

In contrast to the experience with rheumatoid arthritis, the duration of symptoms in osteoarthritis did not influence the degree of relief. The benefits from DMSO were consistently positive regardless of age, length of involvement, or the extent of involvement of the disease process.

The only recorded difference - aside from the occasional individual difference - was that the larger joints, shoulder, hip, knee and in some cases the back, more often required longer treatment to gain maximum benefit.

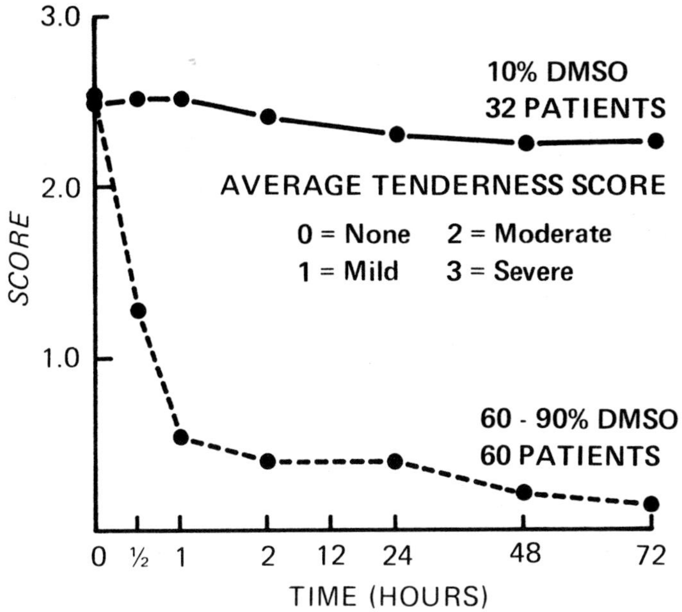

Average tenderness score after double blind study.
Brown: DMSO in Acute Musculoskeletal Conditions (141:502,503).

Some physicians have reported that while using injections of 20% DMSO in 0.5% Xylocaine, they are able to obtain significant benefit sooner than with topical application alone. Many patients prefer the single or multiple injections in the beginning to avoid the inconvenience of topical application with the period of 30 minutes for absorption.

There are both immediate benefits of pain relief and improved joint mobility within 5-20 minutes, and other gradual long-term benefits. The maximum level of long-term benefit occurred in most people within a few months. Long-term relief may be indirect, resulting from the increased activity and mobility allowed by pain relief.

Be aware of the possibility of drug interactions. The least is known about the interaction of DMSO and the newest and most radical of arthritis medications. Other pain relievers and Corticoids may be combined. Since DMSO aids circulation and multiplies the effectiveness of many drugs, less of a particular drug is usually needed to obtain equivalent benefit when combined with DMSO.

Dosage and Application: Each treatment uses one to three teaspoons (5-10 milliliters) of 70%-90% DMSO. This is applied topically to the skin over a large area surrounding the involved joint(s). See the Application Chart.

Repeat applications are most often every 4-6 hours (or 2-4 times daily) in severe attacks. Many find once daily or twice weekly adequate to obtain relief. A few people have reported significant improvement with application every two hours for brief periods.

The only general rule is to **use as needed** in the judgment of the patient to obtain relief.

Once relief is obtained or has peaked, the patient should immediately attempt to reduce usage to discover the minimum dose needed to maintain relief. Maintenance can often be achieved with one treatment now and then - much less frequently.

Chronic sufferers should start more slowly with two treatments per day, five days per week. It is necessary to continue this program for 6-8 weeks before making conclusive evaluations of results. As Dr. Stanley W. Jacob often tells his patients: "DMSO is a slow worker. Don't get discouraged too soon." This is important to emphasize since many have come to expect an immediate response from misleading newspaper reports.

Once maximum relief is obtained the chronic sufferer and user should seek to discover the minimum dose for maximum relief. Read the section on Interval Therapy.

As you may gather from the complications here, it is best to consult with your physician and have him/her supervise and monitor any DMSO therapy for arthritis. Otherwise, you may just end up playing around and not really knowing whether it is, or could be, of benefit to you in the long or short-run.

Topical application is the preferred means of administration of DMSO for arthritis. There is no advantage to oral administration. Application should be to a large, clean area to help the speed of absorption. Wait 15-30 minutes for absorption and wipe off any remaining moisture.

Response: Pain relief and increased joint mobility should occur within 5-20 minutes. For a certain percentage it seems to take longer. Most patients found that after the first few days once or **twice daily** was sufficient to attain the maximum relief and mobility.

There was increasing evidence that, at least for many, **once or twice weekly** is an excellent maintenance dose. Sometimes previously persistent symptoms disappeared for from five days to three weeks without additional treatment. This has been referred to as "carry-over effect."

Special Precaution: Long-term users should experiment to find the least amount and frequency of DMSO to gain the desired relief. As an added precaution against any potential long-term toxic effects, consider "the five days on and two days off" weekly schedule, with two weeks every six months without any DMSO. This could potentially allow the body to make any needed adjustment which the DMSO might otherwise be preventing. Be particularly careful when using DMSO long-term in conjunction with other medication. Consult your physician or pharmacist for advice.

DMSO in Gout

The first attack of gout, which occurs typically in the large toe, is dramatically reduced by topical application of DMSO. Later occurrences don't respond as well, and the more frequent the attacks the less helpful DMSO appears to be. Nonetheless, a significant number of long-term sufferers feel DMSO usually provides valuable relief.

Keep in mind that most attacks of gout can be prevented by dietary restrictions and/or with specific gout medications.

Dosage and Application: Apply topically to the affected area and its surroundings as needed for pain relief - more at first, and less as relief is obtained.

Response: Pain relief occurs in about 30 minutes. This is an acute condition and should resolve completely within 48 hours. Residual discomfort can, of course, be treated with an occasional application of DMSO.

Bursitis

Bursae are small sacs of connective tissue usually interposed between tendons, ligaments and bones. Bursae function as lubricating buffers between moving parts, facilitating the passage of muscles or tendons over bony or ligamentous surfaces. Minor bursae occur between skin and bone and where tendons cross over or overlay bony projections. There are approximately 1000 bursae in the human body.

Bursitis is inflammation of the bursae, usually caused by excess stress or tension placed on the bursae, or from some local or systemic inflammatory process. Bursitis may be acute or chronic. The acute form is disabling, the involved area being swollen, tender and very painful in motion. With chronic bursitis, the shoulder can actually become stiff, even though the joint itself is not diseased. Occasionally, a calcium deposit also is present. If bursitis persists, the muscles eventually atrophy.

CLINICAL EFFECT OF DMSO: TRAUMATIC INJURIES (732 CASES)

Type of Injury	No. of Cases	Partial Remission of Symptoms	Complete Remission of Symptoms	Failures
Sprains, strains, contusions	479	95	325	59
Fractures (postoperative treatment)	147	39	88	20
Meniscus injuries	39	10	21	8
Burns (grades 1,2)	4	—	3	1
Posttraumatic and postoperative pain	63	14	36	13
		21.6%	64.6%	13.8%

John and Laudahn: *Clinical Experiences of DMSO* (141:508)

Bursitis may occur in any of the bursae, but the most frequent location is the subacromial bursae in the shoulder. Because the subacromial bursae is close to the shoulder joint, inflammation of this bursae makes movement of the shoulder joint limited and painful. The supraspinatus tendon forms the floor of the subacromial bursae; the patient with subacromial bursitis has limited ability to raise the arm away from the body. Eventually, with inflammation, deposits of calcium occur in the supraspinatus tendon, and further interferes with shoulder motion. Other common sites of bursitis are the subdeltoid bursae in the shoulder joint, the olecranon bursae of the elbow, and the prepatellar bursae of the knee.

Conventional treatment for bursitis is usually confined to immobilization of the affected area, followed by gradually progressing exercises.

Dosage and Application: The most commonly reported approach for both acute and chronic bursitis has been two to three teaspoons (10-15 milliliters) of 70%-90% DMSO applied topically two to four times per day until initial relief is obtained (always within 24 hours). Frequency of treatment can then be decreased rapidly over a period of about eight days for acute, and up to several weeks or months in chronic cases.

Application should cover a large, clean area. Wait 15-30 minutes for absorption and wipe off any remaining moisture. See Application Chart.

Special Precaution: When applying DMSO to the shoulder area, the subject should refrain from the use of anti-perspirant. There are some relatively toxic substances in most anti-perspirants and these are likely to penetrate more readily during DMSO therapy. (In fact, a fair portion of most underarm anti-perspirants penetrate in any case.)

Response: Bursitis is one of the conditions in which DMSO is most effective. Response rates for all researchers ran at about 90 percent with a good-to-excellent response.

Acute bursitis is most often reported to completely subside without recurrence. In many of these instances, it is proper to speak of DMSO as a cure. In most other applications, it is appropriately referred to as a treatment for certain symptoms.

Chronic cases often required repeated applications. Other researchers suggest lasting benefit only after a treatment period of weeks to a few months. Calcium deposits seem to disappear in varying lengths of time, from a few days to several weeks.

Several researchers report that following two or three applications, most patients experience a regression of pain and muscular spasm, and a marked improvement in the mobility of joints. Some of them were able to move their joints without pain, one half to one hour following the first application.

Even in cases of frozen shoulder (less than 50% mobility): "One application of DMSO resulted in the patient being able to institute almost complete range of motion without discomfort. **It should be emphasized that one application did not cure the entity but benefit seen from one treatment was dramatic**. (Paul, 141:591)."

John and Laudahn, who reported results of treating over 1000 cases of bursitis (293 acute, 782 chronic), comment, "A 50-year old patient had suffered from a therapy resistent subacromial of the left shoulder for three months and could abduct (lift) his left arm only a little and with great pain.

Twenty minutes following the first application he was able to raise the affected arm with almost no pain. The regression and disappearance of calcification, which had been observed for as long as seven months to several years, regressed after DMSO therapy of several weeks duration. (141:510)." Reports of disappearance of calcification were documented by X-rays and came from several independent researchers.

There are clearly some patients who do not respond. "We noticed that those who do respond to DMSO do so upon the first or second application. It is our impression that when patients respond, the length of therapy time is decreased and the patient is more comfortable during therapy." (Parsons, Shepard, and Fosdick, 141:569.)

Tendonitis and Peritendonitis

Tendons are connective tissue structures connecting the muscles with their skeletal supports. They are composed of parallel white fibers closely bound into bundles, between which the living cells of the tendon are compressed. The entire tendon is surrounded by a membranous sheath. Normally, there is a small amount of synovial fluid in the sheath to provide lubrication. Aponeuroses, ligaments and fasciae are fibrous structures resembling tendons in structure. The first are broadly expanded and usually bind down muscles. The second connect bones. The third are fibrous coverings of muscles and other organs.

"Tendonitis" means literally an inflammation of the tendons. The condition is characterized by inflammation of the tendons and their investing sheaths, and is a common cause of pain due to inflammation of the muscle covers (fasciae). Tendonitis and peritendonitis ("peri" means around or surrounding) can occur anywhere in the body, but is found particularly in the region of the shoulder, elbow, wrist, knee and ankle. It is usually due to single and reported trauma, or may follow excessive use of the tendon.

Dosage and Application: Topical applications of one to three teaspoons (5-15 milliliters) of 70%-90% DMSO are given every 4-6 hours, or up to four times per day in the beginning. Once relief is obtained, frequency of treatment can be decreased rapidly. Length of treatment required depends on severity and underlying causes. The reported periods range from three days to nine months.

Application should cover a large, clean area. Wait 15-30 minutes for absorption and wipe off any remaining moisture. See Application Chart.

Response: The onset of response is rapid - 10 to 15 minutes - and the duration of response about four hours. The frequency of applications can be decreased after the first few days, and the duration of treatment is relatively short. One researcher, in a study of several musculoskeletal conditions reported, "The most favorable results were obtained in this condition, with a response of 94. (Steinberg, 141:536.)"

Sports Injuries

Acute musculoskeletal injuries commonly associated with physically stressful sports activities respond extremely well to treatment with DMSO.

Soft-tissue injuries, including sprains of the various joints and back, strains and twists of muscles and supporting structures, bruises, both of the soft tissue and of the bone, most kinds of inflammation of muscles and associated tissues, have all benefited from DMSO treatment, either as the primary therapy or as an adjunct.

In its action as a skeletal muscle relaxant (anti-cholinesterase), DMSO appears to be the treatment of choice for muscle spasms and many sorts of cramps. Research has found that DMSO helped reduce the initial trauma, as well as providing significant aid in healing injuries involving tendons, cartilage, and ligaments. In cases of cracks, chips and major fractures of bones, DMSO treatment reduces initial swelling, facilitates healing processes, and aids in recovery of full function.

The beneficial effects of DMSO in this wide range of conditions can be traced to several primary phenomena:

1. Relieves pain.
2. Reduces inflammation.
3. Reduces swelling.
4. Promotes circulation.
5. Prevents "clumping" of cellular debris.

This list could be easily expanded, for instance, by adding that DMSO "helps to restore normal functioning (metabolism) of cells and tissues following injury." However, you could just as easily reduce the list to three primary actions: pain relief, promotion of circulation, and anti-inflammatory effect.

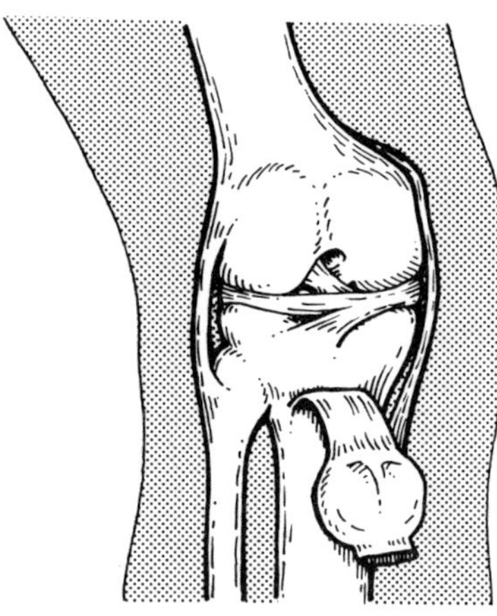

A Special Look at Mechanisms

Pain relief has secondary consequences that follow mostly from increased mobility. Movement of an injury area, or at least the associated limb, is often quite valuable to both healing and recovery. But even without its analgesic effect, DMSO would be important in sports medicine for its promotion of circulation. It is this that leads to a reduction in swelling and restoration of normal cellular functioning in the area of injury.

Without proper circulation bringing oxygen and other nutrients and removing toxic cellular debris, the damage cycle often continues for some hours at the site of an injury. Recent studies in spinal cord injuries suggest that cellular death is often not finalized for hours after the initial trauma - even when the spinal cord is completely severed! More cells are damaged or destroyed by later starvation and toxic side effects than by the initial trauma.

The "clumping" of the cellular debris from initially damaged cells tends to clog the microcirculation. This is a major cause of the swelling. By preventing or reversing this aggregation of debris, the DMSO prevents and/or reduces swelling at the site of an injury. (Some people might argue that to call the anti-aggregation effect a promotion of circulation effect is stretching the word a little.)

There is no reason to believe that swelling is beneficial - "the body's natural response to injury." From all we know, swelling doesn't help anything. For many years the first-line response to traumatic injury has been to use ice packs and mineral salt baths to reduce or prevent swelling. Moreover, the use of heat in various forms appears to be effective, primarily to promote circulation, particularly the microcirculation.

From all we can learn, there is no reason to believe that the cellular debris should remain at the site of injury. There is no benefit. The numerous phagocytic (debris eating) cells are located throughout the body, and are perfectly capable of handling large influxes from the site of injury.

Action During the Healing Process

DMSO also seems to be helpful **during** the healing process. Many believe this effect is, again, traceable to the effect on the circulation.

Having perhaps over-emphasized the role of the promotion of the circulation, it remains to mention the anti-inflammatory effect. Some of the anti-inflammatory effects of DMSO can clearly be attributed to the improvement brought about through adequate circulation. However, it is likely that DMSO's anti-oxidant activity, its stabilization of lysosomes, and its action as a radical scavenger are all important in producing positive benefits in sports injuries. Many health problems in sports medicine are due primarily to irritation and subsequent inflammation. In these cases, the anti-inflammatory action of DMSO may become the principal source of benefit.

Besides the benefits that occur when DMSO is applied at the time of a sports injury, and during the healing process, there is the potential for further benefits, if DMSO is applied in anticipation - when an injury begins to develop - as well as much later during the recovery phase. By reducing pain and aiding full circulation, DMSO can help in the recovery process after primary healing is complete.

By now, there are an extremely large number of positive anecdotal stories from athletes about the wonders of DMSO. These run from the early story about Daryl Lamonica's jammed thumb, to the more recent stories of the frequent applications of DMSO by two-time New York Marathon winner, Alberto Salazar.

A rough survey suggested 10% of athletes had dramatic positive results, 70% good-to-excellent, and 20% no benefit. About a quarter of this last group (5% of the original total) stopped treatment because of side effects - usually the skin rash. Those who otherwise do not benefit appear to be randomly distributed (unpredictable) - they do not show any obvious common characteristic.

Selected Case Reports

The following are some selected comments of the medical researchers themselves:

"Eight players of the Buffalo Bills football team were treated with this drug during the 1964 season. During play, it is only natural that acute muscular trauma occurs. In each case, the player returned to full duty 50% sooner than he would with other forms of therapy. These injuries included severe muscular contraction of the adduction thigh muscles, acutely strained sternomastoid muscle, acute sprain of sternoclavicular joint, and another with acute sprain of medial collateral ligaments of the knee. In four other patients, low back injuries responded in 50% of the expected period of disability." (Lockie and Norcross, 141:601.)

Drs. Lockie and Norcross were located in the Department of Medicine at the State University of New York at Buffalo when this research was undertaken. The results of treatment of 103 such patients are summarized in their report, (141:599-602).

"In treating acute injuries, no comparison was made with a controlled group, and admittedly, DMSO was given only twice a week; however, the author has had considerable experience with this type of injury am physician of the Toronto Mapleleafs. These were not the types of acute disability that ordinarily respond rapidly. A favorable response to dimethylsulfoxide was considered unequivocal.

"In each case, graded 'excellent' or 'good,' the response to DMSO substantially shortened the period of disability of such injuries when compared with those treated by rest, physical therapy, phenylbutazone, analgesics, etc.

"P.M., a 24-year-old male 'Olympic type' runner, strained his groin muscles two months prior to DMSO therapy. One week following one application of DMSO, this patient was able to run a mile in his normal clocked time. He had been athletically incapacitated for two months before treatment, in spite of physical therapy, rest and analgesics.

"D.C., a 27-year-old male office employee, entered with a severe cervical (neck) muscle strain. The patient exhibited torticollis (definition of torticollis: Wryneck: a contracted state of the cervical muscles producing twisting of the neck and an unnatural position of the head).

"M.A., a 20-year-old professional baseball player, sustained a severe injury to his ankle. In the era before DMSO was used as a therapeutic agent the author would have placed his ankle in a cast for several weeks. DMSO was applied and the ankle was measured both before and one half hour after treatment. There was, by actual measurement, a quarter of an inch reduction in the girth one half hour following DMSO therapy. DMSO was reapplied twice, and within one week this patient was able to compete in professional baseball with only minimal disability." (Paul, 141:590.)

CLINICAL EFFECT OF DMSO: ACUTE AND CHRONIC MUSCULOSKELETAL DISORDERS (3321 CASES)

	No. of Cases	Maximum Period of Treatment (Months)	Partial Remission of Symptoms	Complete Remission of Symptoms	Failures
1. Bursitis, periarthritis (1075)					
a) acute	293	1	121	136	36
b) chronic	782	3	321	345	116
2. Periostitis, epicondylitis Tendinitis	409	2	111	238	60
3. Osteoarthritis (1641)					
a) spine	896	2	253	539	104
b) hip	104	6	52	28	24
c) knee	497	6	202	215	80
d) small joints	144	3	46	69	29
4. Rheumatoid arthritis (grades 1,2)	177	6	68	74	35
5. Gouty arthritis	19	2	3	16	—
			35.4%	50.0%	14.6%

John and Laudahn: *Clinical Experiences of DMSO* (141:509)

Note: The reader should note that Dr. Paul's approach in all these cases was to use what he refers to as "interval therapy": DMSO applied only once or twice a week. See the discussion of "Interval Therapy" elsewhere in the book. Paul's work was done in cooperation with Merck, Sharp and Dohme of Canada Limited, and covered 180 patients.

"I have been impressed with the dramatic and striking results obtained with DMSO in acute musculoskeletal and soft tissue problems, both traumatic and non-traumatic. Treatment of these conditions, in my experience, has been so successful and strikingly productive of relief of pain, tenderness and muscle spasms, and in the restoration of limited motion, that it has been extremely difficult to return to what I now feel is antedated treatment, namely all analgesics, muscular relaxants, tranquilizers, corticosteroids, and physical therapy. While treating patients with DMSO, I discarded the use of elastic bandaging, adhesive taping and splinting supports for soft tissue injuries. The gratitude of these patients was substantial, particularly since results were so promptly noticed. Incapacity was substantially lessened and work time loss strikingly mitigated. In acute sprain to the extremities and low back and acute soft tissue injuries, with associated subcutaneous bleeding, skin discoloration and edema (swelling), DMSO was definitely established to be the treatment of choice.

"There were disadvantages in the side effects and in the length of time required for the patient to apply medication and to allow for absorption, but pain relief and symptomatic improvement were so striking that the average patient accepted these inconveniences." ((J. Harold Brown, M.D., 141:504-505); Brown's clinical investigations covered ten months and involved over 250 patients. This work was undertaken in cooperation with Merck, Sharp, and Dohme through its Research Laboratories.)

Dosage and Application: Most reports suggest topical application of one to three teaspoons (5-15 milliliters) of 70%-90% DMSO every four-six hours, or two to four times per day in the beginning. As relief is obtained, the frequency of treatment can be decreased rapidly. Length of treatment depends on the nature and severity of the condition. The majority of acute cases were able to cease using DMSO within a week. Others required or chose to continue for several weeks or months. Those considering an extended period of treatment should consider adopting the five days on, two days off routine. Keep in mind that in at least one study twice weekly DMSO treatments achieved results comparable to more frequent application.

Application should cover a large, clean area, including and surrounding the area of concern. Wait 15-30 minutes for absorption and wipe off any remaining moisture.

Response: Pain may be expected to diminish within 10-15 minutes and the effect will last about four to six hours. Swelling has been reported to reduce significantly within one half hour. Control of inflammation should be amply apparent within 48 hours.

Results were similar in both athletes and non-athletes. It appears that the level of physical fitness and age, prior to DMSO therapy, was not a factor in benefit or lack of benefit from DMSO. (Paul, 141:587).

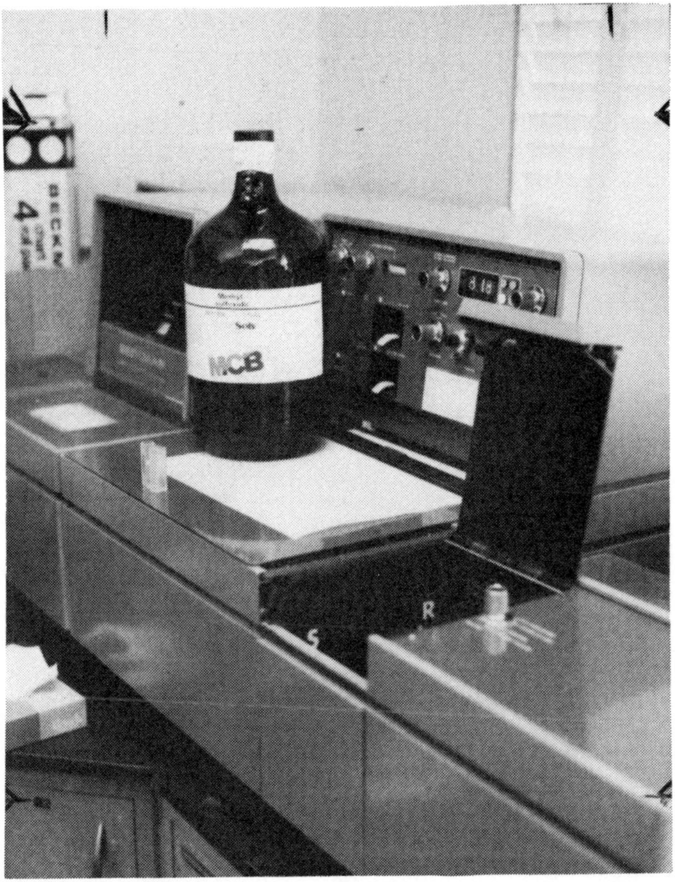
MCB

6

SPECIFIC APPLICATIONS – II

Pain

Treating Pain

Among all the demonstrated therapeutic benefits of DMSO, its ability to reduce or eliminate pain stands out from all the rest. The effectiveness of DMSO as an analgesic (pain reliever) in many conditions is unquestioned. As a rule, the effect is dramatic within 5-10 minutes, but may occasionally require more than 20 minutes for full potency. DMSO has been referred to as the aspirin of the 21st Century. The main difference between aspirin and DMSO, therapeutically at least, is that DMSO is much **less** toxic.

According to one hypothesis, DMSO and aspirin may act on pain by the same mechanism - by altering the production of certain chemical activators called prostaglandins. Aspirin, however, has various other side effects not found with DMSO.

We do know that DMSO does not work the same as narcotic pain relievers. One recent series of experiments compared DMSO to morphine. The researchers first established that DMSO was an equally potent and longer lasting pain reliever than morphine. Second, they used the narcotic-blocker naloxone, which interferes with the pain-relieving action of morphine type drugs. An injection of naloxone prevented any pain relief in the morphine, but left unchanged the pain-relieving qualities of DMSO.

This is not entirely surprising, since we have known for some time that no narcotic-like dependence ever develops with DMSO. Furthermore, the body builds a tolerance to narcotic pain-relievers, necessitating larger and larger doses over time. This does not occur with DMSO. In fact, in chronic pain situations, there is evidence the amount and frequency of DMSO needed to maintain pain relief - once maximum relief has been attained - actually decreases over time. The "carryover" effect, where previously chronic pain does not return even after DMSO is stopped, may run up to five weeks.

Narcotic pain-relievers often have significant long-term side effects, including an impairment of digestive functioning and constipation. DMSO doesn't have these side effects.

DMSO and aspirin are alike in that they have both local and systemic effects. In other words, if you apply DMSO to a specific site of pain, you will gain faster and better relief than if you apply it elsewhere. Thus, it is preferable to apply it near the site of pain. However, DMSO applied anywhere on the body, or even taken orally, will produce a pain-relieving effect at localized sites.

Dosage and Application: In general, apply one to three teaspoons (5-15 milliliters) of 70%-90% DMSO as needed to obtain, and then maintain, pain relief. Typically, applications are as frequent as every two hours in severely acute situations. This usually tapers off to one application every four to six hours. Often relief can be maintained with once a day or twice a week applications.

When applying DMSO for pain, cover a large area, including the site of the problem. The area should be clean. Allow 15-30 minutes for the DMSO to absorb. Wipe off the excess moisture at the end of this period.

Response: In acute cases, initial relief is obtained in 5-15 minutes and lasts approximately 4-6 hours. In chronic cases, the relief is less complete and maximum relief takes longer.

The benefits of DMSO in chronic pain relief may be obtained with only once or twice a week treatments in combination with other pain relief medications. DMSO operates to deliver the other medications more efficiently.

Neuritis and Neuralgia

Neuritis is a nerve inflammation and occurs normally in a single nerve. The causes are usually either physical trauma, extension of some other inflammation, such as herpes (for example, in shingles), injection of chemical irritants, poor blood flow or chilling. This is a general term and can include problems with either central nerves or those extending furthest away from the spinal area (for instance, sciatica involves inflammation of the sciatic nerve(s) extending into the leg).

Neuralgia is another general term and means literally nerve pain. Pain in these cases can be either sharp and sudden as in trigeminal neuralgia or tic douloureux, or dull and chronic. The nature of the pain is often an excellent indication of the nature of the underlying problem. You should always contact your physician to secure an accurate diagnosis. Whenever possible, it is much wiser to correct the underlying problem (which may get worse) rather than being tied to regular use of analgesics.

Dosage and Application: Research reports suggest that topical application of one to three teaspoons (5-15 milliliters) of 70%-90% DMSO is a successful approach. Applications can be made two-four times daily, as needed, to obtain or maintain relief. As in other conditions, once initial relief is obtained, the frequency of applications can usually be reduced - for instance, to once or twice per week.

When applying the DMSO, cover a large area, including the site of the problem, if this can be determined. The area should be clean. Allow 15-30 minutes for DMSO to absorb. Wipe off the excess moisture when finished.

Response: Certainly in the acute cases, initial relief occurs in 5-15 minutes, and the total period of treatment is usually between two to five days. In more involved conditions, the treatment period may extend up to two to three weeks.

The more chronic the condition, the less complete is the relief and maximum relief takes longer. Also, the more involved conditions, in general, seem to gain less overall relief, both in the short term and the long term; in the good-to-excellent, fewer "excellent" and more "goods." Chronic sufferers do report - if less than complete - long-term relief. DMSO allows the chronic sufferer to reduce the dosage of other analgesics.

DMSO is not a panacea, but in many of these cases, it is clearly worth trying. Many patients experience traumatic relief for conditions that have persisted for years despite other attempted therapies and surgeries. The research reports vary in overall response in this area: 50%-90% good-to-excellent.

Back Pain and Neck Pain

Back pain can have several underlying causes that we know about. Various strains or sprains or muscle spasms lead up to the more serious degenerative disc disease where the vertebral discs begin to deteriorate. For some, the pain is localized, and others have pain radiating into the hips, buttock or legs. The benefit following DMSO in degenerative disc disease may be due to its relaxant effect on the skeletal musculature.

Discussing a group with degenerative lumbar disc disease, Paul comments: "This group all showed X-ray evidence of narrowed intervertebral spaces. The natural history of degenerative lumbar disc disease, aided by traditional medical therapy of analgesics, fracture boards, heat, etc., is a self-limiting one. Usually with the aforementioned measures, the attack subsides within a few weeks. DMSO therapy in the vast majority in a series of 25 patients, resulted in a significantly shorter period of disability. In some of the patients, two or three applications of DMSO, followed by almost total symptomatic relief. The mechanism of benefit is not well understood (141:593)."

Paul also reported on a group with degenerative cervical (neck) disc disease, and included the following case report. "One patient with an acute whiplash injury, a male aged 52, is included in this group. The result following treatment with DMSO was considered good. Four applications (over two weeks) of DMSO, produced more benefit in this patient than the cervical collar, analgesics, muscle relaxants, and physiotherapy which he had received in the five weeks before DMSO (141:593)." This should not be taken to be a typical case, but it is a significant indicator of what might be expected potentially in some cases.

Dosage and Application: Best results have occurred with topical application of one to three teaspoons (5-15 milliliters) of 70%-90% DMSO, two to four times daily, or as needed, to obtain or maintain relief. Maximum pain relief, in the beginning, lasts about four to six hours. Once initial relief is obtained, the frequency of applications can usually be greatly reduced, for instance, to once or twice per week. Total treatment time, in a few cases, ranges from 5 to 25 days. In chronic cases, relief continued with repeated applications.

Treatment of degenerative disc disease was one area where DMSO was used in conjunction with ultrasound therapy. The ultrasound was applied immediately after topical application of the DMSO. This helped the DMSO penetrate more rapidly and generally increased speed of initial pain relief from 15-20 minutes down to 5-10 minutes. The overall judgment was that DMSO and ultrasound therapy worked well together.

The area of application should be clean. Cover a large area, including and surrounding the site of the problem. Allow 15-30 minutes for the DMSO to absorb. Wipe off the excess moisture when finished.

Topical Application Chart — II

Cover a large area surrounding the neck or lower back, as indicated.

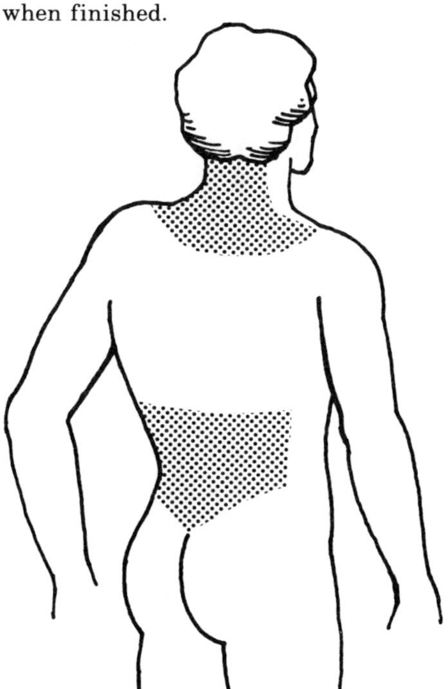

Response: Pain relief occurs typically within 10-30 minutes. This lasts four to six hours in the acute phase, but may extend for much greater periods once the problem is under control. One researcher reported: "Two patients had long required regular doses of narcotics to obtain any comfort or sleep. They were able to discontinue their narcotics completely while on DMSO. Both continued relatively comfortable for approximately one month after treatment was stopped (in 1965 due to the FDA ban), and then had a flare-up of their severe pain. This 'carryover effect' was seen in other patients and ranged from several days to five weeks (Blumenthal and Fuchs, 141:577)." (This was the original discovery of the "carryover effect.")

Overall response was much greater (90%) in those suffering their first severe attack of lower back pain. The more recurrent the condition, the less the response (70%). Neck pain and cervical disc disease conditions showed as low as a 60%-70% response in the good-to-excellent range in some studies.

Headache

There is considerable variety in the causes and personal histories of headaches. The main studies of DMSO for headache distinguish three types of headache: vascular, tension and post-traumatic.

External nerve pain in the head and neck region are classified as cases of neuralgia. Many cases of arthritis and disc disease, which may in fact, include headache as a secondary symptom, are not necessarily included here. However, many headaches in these latter classifications can be viewed as part of the category of chronic post-traumatic headaches. Headaches primarily associated with sinusitis, because of their special cause, nature and responsiveness, are treated separately.

Vascular headaches, including migraine and cluster, are characterized by a dilation of the blood vessels in some area of the head. The specific cause or mechanism producing the pain is not well understood.

Tension headaches are understood as due to anxiety, tension, or other psychological or emotional conflict. Included here are also those headaches stemming from generalized muscle spasm or contraction of the skeletal muscles at the back of the head and neck.

Post-traumatic headaches are separated into acute and chronic. These trace back one way or another to some specific injury.

Three different research studies report on DMSO for vascular headaches. The response claims vary from 40% good-to-excellent to 100% (10 out of 10) good-to-excellent. (The latter study was undertaken in association with Squibb Institute for Medical Research.) The sizes of these studies are small, so it is difficult to draw any definite conclusions one way or another. DMSO is certainly not universally successful for migraines; however, a significant group do obtain benefit.

DMSO is very successful in the treatment of tension headaches. Almost all of these anxiety and psychologic headaches have associated spasm of muscles in the head and neck. Much of the relief obtained in these cases is probably due to the reaction of DMSO as a relaxant for skeletal muscles.

In headaches classified as post-traumatic, there is considered to be an underlying physical cause tracing back to a single accident or injury episode, or to an area of repeated minor irritational stress. Degenerative disc disease is typical of this latter category. Headaches following acute injuries, even though they may have persisted for some time, appear to respond to DMSO better than any other single category headache. As in other conditions, the more chronic and recurrent the problem, the less DMSO seems to help, and thus will most likely take longer to gain maximum benefit. Still, many people in this latter group gained significant benefits, where other therapies failed.

Dosage and Application: Topical application of 70%-90% DMSO to the forehead and back of the head is most common. One teaspoon (5 milliliters) is adequate in most instances, unless there is a need to cover a larger area over the shoulders, when up to three teaspoons (15 milliliters) might be used. The frequency can be up to two to four times daily depending on what is needed to obtain and maintain relief.

Research suggests that application to hairy areas such as the scalp is all right. However, anyone using hair dye or hair conditioners that remain on the hair would be wise to avoid this practice. For those who are balding, the most effective place to apply the DMSO may be to the top of the head.

Total treatment time is usually one day, with repeated applications for recurrence, as necessary.

There is some indication that the more quickly DMSO is applied from the first sign of a headache, the quicker and better the results.

Response: In roughly half the cases, relief is obtained within 10 minutes. Almost everyone who claimed benefit experienced it within one half hour. Often one application is sufficient to terminate that particular headache episode.

Based on a summary of research reports, it is possible to project an estimate that between 60%-90% of headache sufferers will find DMSO to be an effective treatment. Many people report DMSO worked well as an adjunct to other medications. It is often claimed that narcotic analgesics could be reduced by half or more when using DMSO.

Some patients are able to anticipate the onset of a recurring type of headache. DMSO can be used in these cases to prevent headache for periods of months.

As a general rule, acute headaches respond better than chronic.

SPECIFIC APPLICATIONS – III

7

Burns

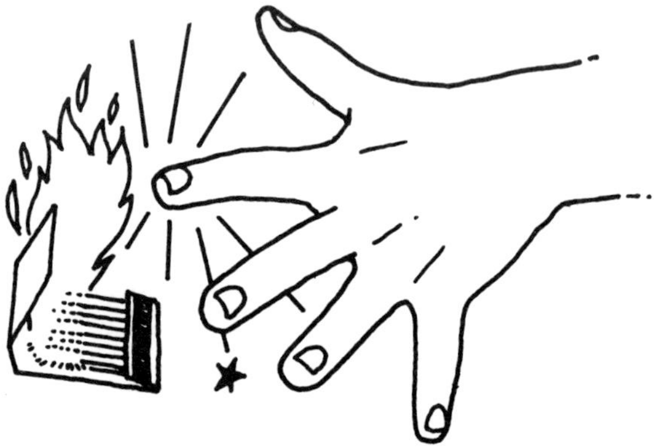

There is very little research published about DMSO therapy for burns. Given what we know about DMSO in other conditions, it is natural to expect important benefits in first, second and third degree burns. One might expect pain relief, anti-inflammatory effect, reduction of swelling and improved healing time. All these benefits have been reported by someone or for some group of patients.

We are aware of one major animal study that was undertaken at the University of Oregon Medical School, but the results were never published. Conveniently, one of the research assistants in that study is now on the staff of The DMSO News Service. The results were uniformly positive in all aspects. Stated most concisely: "One thing - it works." DMSO was compared to other standard burn therapies, such as silver nitrate, sulfa-type drugs and peroxide. DMSO outperformed all others. In particular, 100% DMSO stopped blistering and served to dehydrate the burn area. Treated once or twice daily, the healing time was "significantly reduced."

The most complete clinical report on human trials comes from a study by Goldman in 1965 in association with Merck and Company and Syntex Corporation. "The most striking and gratifying results with DMSO were obtained in three patients with first and second degree burns of the hands. The first application of 70% aqueous DMSO uniformly and dramatically relieved pain within a few minutes, promptly dried the lesions, and resulted in healing in one-half to two-thirds the time it usually takes with the more conventional methods of treatment. Only one application at the time of the burn, and another on the following day were sufficient to effect complete relief of pain and drying of the denuded areas. One half hour after the use of DMSO a dry, sterile dressing was applied (Goldman, 141:653)."

The sooner DMSO was applied after the burn episode, the better the overall benefit. Several clinicians have reported that they have used 100% DMSO for superficial burns with excellent results. This is one of the few times 100% DMSO seems preferable over 90% DMSO. The most immediate benefit is pain relief, which may take 5-15 minutes, however. DMSO appears to prevent blistering in many cases, and prevents the otherwise frequent loss of skin at the site of the burn.

There are indications that if DMSO is applied quickly, within the first few minutes, a great deal of the damage can be prevented. This is because DMSO is a powerful anti-oxidant. Oxidation of tissue during this initial period is a major aspect of the damage process.

Although all we have is anecdotal information, we feel it is reasonable to mention that there have been a number of reliable reports of the value of DMSO in treatment of both mild and severe sunburn.

Dosage and Application: For superficial burns apply 90%-100% DMSO topically as quickly as possible. Cover an area larger than the actual burn site. "If you burn your finger-tip on the stove just dip it in a bottle of 100% DMSO for a few seconds." Five to 15 milliliters of DMSO spread over a large, cleansed area should be adequate for all but the largest burns. Remember that the effects of DMSO are systemic, therefore, there is no need to soak every local affected area. After the first application apply every four-six hours, as needed, to maintain pain relief. For healing, it appears that two or three applications during the first two days may be sufficient.

There should be no problem in applying any other normal burn ointment or cream, either before or after using DMSO.

Response: Pain relief should occur within five-ten minutes. This lasts about four-six hours. Total treatment period rarely extends beyond one week.

Frostbite

DMSO appears to be the solution to frostbite. Someday, everyone moving in conditions of severe cold and/or wind chill will carry a small bottle of DMSO. There are no published clinical studies on humans, but several physicians have submitted brief case reports, claiming dramatic success.

There has been a major animal study using DMSO to prevent and treat frostbite. Animals treated with DMSO prior to being subjected to a tissue freeze incident showed a "welt" just like the untreated. However, in the DMSO-treated animals, the welt would disappear within hours, or a day or two at most. In the untreated animals, the welt would develop into a significant wound with loss of skin and tissue and so forth, taking weeks to heal.

DMSO applied very soon after a cold-burn or tissue freeze incident appears to be almost as effective as pre-treatment. In the human cases that were treated up to 24 hours after the freeze incident, there was complete recovery of tissue without loss of skin.

None of this should be surprising since the first major use of DMSO in biological setting was as an anti-freeze preservative for tissue. DMSO is currently used extensively in the freeze-preservation of (1) sperm and eggs associated with artificial insemination, (2) red and white blood cell preservation for later transfusions, and (3) a variety of tissues, including small pieces of important glands and bone marrow for later transplantation.

Dosage and Application: Treatment in the animal study and in the human case reports was 70%-90% DMSO twice daily for up to a week. There is good reason to believe that much less frequent applications will be just as effective. One to three teaspoons (5 to 15 milliliters) of DMSO solution should be used, depending on the size of the area to be covered.

In an acute situation, where the DMSO is applied **after** the freeze incident, a soak would be appropriate.

Apply the DMSO to a clean area and allow 15-30 minutes for it to absorb.

Special Precaution: A physician we spoke with who has had experience with DMSO in frostbite, and highly recommends it, posed the following dilemma. In many situations, it will be inappropriate to expose the hands or feet for 15-30 minutes while the DMSO absorbs. There is some danger that when DMSO-wet hands are placed in mittens or gloves, and feet in socks, that the dye from the materials will be carried through the skin.

There is good reason to believe that these dyes will not penetrate any more than the first layer of skin and don't pose a serious danger (although some irritation could result). The dye molecules are usually too large for even DMSO to help them through the skin. However, in general, the situation should be avoided.

Alternatively, one could apply the DMSO to the lower leg instead of to the foot and to the lower arm instead of the hands. This should be nearly as effective, certainly as a preventative measure. This may or may not help to solve the dilemma depending on the clothing. Using 90% DMSO will shorten the time needed for the DMSO to absorb.

Covering the area of application with a plastic sheet of polyethylene (please **not** polyvinylchloride, PVC) will also solve the problem. Some enterprising soul should have thin plastic (polyethylene or polyurethane) gloves and socks made, to be sold in skiing and mountaineering outlets. A small amount of DMSO could then be applied, covered with the plastic glove or sock, and then placed in the regular glove or sock.

Response: Any pain should disappear in 10-15 minutes. The DMSO will clear the area of microscopic debris and help to restore normal cellular function by returning adequate blood supply. The healing should be dramatically improved, and the healing time shortened. The benefits should be so great that you will doubt whether you ever actually had any true tissue freezing.

Sinusitis

The most frequent medical complaint in the United States is sinusitis. Most generally understood, this means an inflammation of one of the sinuses above the nose. A more restricted definition of sinusitis requires the demonstration of an actual infection of one of the sinuses. Because of the resulting blockage of normal mucus flow, pressure builds and this, together with the inflammatory process can produce headache and severe discomfort.

DMSO is reported to be better than 95% effective in reducing the inflammation, restoring normal mucus flow and relieving the headache and discomfort.

Dosage and Application: Two approaches to treating sinusitis have proved effective. One is to apply 70%-90% DMSO topically (externally) over the sinuses. These are located around the eyes. (There is no added danger in applying DMSO in the vicinity of the eyes.)

The second approach is to use nose drops of a 10%-30% DMSO solution. A cotton swab can be used to coat the inside of the nostril.

In both approaches the total application is usually no greater than one teaspoon of DMSO solution. One or two applications is usually effective, although a repeat application may be helpful four-six hours later.

Special Precaution: Don't apply any DMSO to mucous membranes (nose, mouth, eyes, anus, genitals) in concentrations above 30% DMSO. Because of the delicate nature of these tissues, the moist surface and the interplay of DMSO with water, the lesser concentration is quite enough and effective. Irritation of the mucous surfaces is more likely with higher concentrations of DMSO.

Response: The external approach is less radical, takes longer (10-30 minutes) and avoids irritating already sensitive mucous membranes. The 30% DMSO nose drop approach has been described as similar to applying a ".45 calibre automatic pistol" to solve the problem. It is effective but can be painful for the first few minutes. Several applications of a 10% DMSO solution will probably be just as effective and less painful.

A typical response is pain relief within five-ten minutes followed by decreased nasal congestion and profuse nasal discharge within one half hour. Acute sinus pain itself is reported to be "easily relieved" with DMSO.

Chronic sinusitis sufferers can expect less complete relief. A few chronic sufferers get no relief.

Paul reports the following case study: "The response in one patient was particularly impressive. This 52-year-old female had had recurrent nasal polyps and in an attempt to treat this entity she had been subjected to many polypectomies, which all proved to be unsuccessful. In desperation, she was subjected to a course of radiation therapy, but again, this was unsuccessful. Following topical DMSO therapy, using the patient's own words, 'DMSO had done more' for this recurring condition than any other type of therapy previously tried. A few minutes after DMSO was applied to the patient, a large volume of purulent (containing pus) material drained from the nose and relief of congestion occurred (Paul, 141:594)."

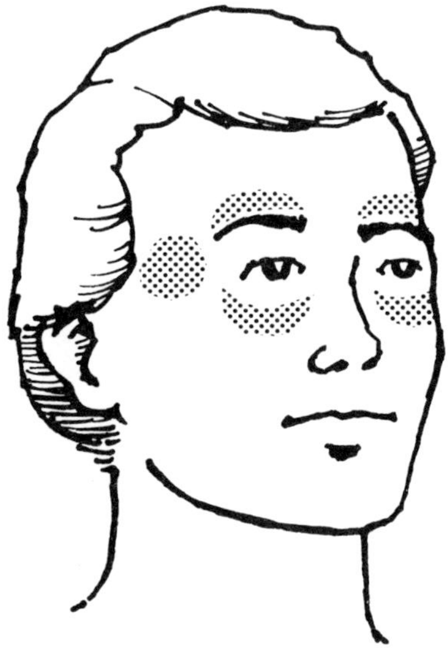

Topical Application Chart

Cover the area surrounding the sinuses.

Peripheral Circulatory Disease

This category of problems is primarily composed of (1) cases of arteriosclerosis, where circulation to the extremities (arms and/or legs) is seriously restricted, and (2) cases of circulatory muscle spasm, where contraction of the muscular layer of the arteries closes off blood flow - particularly in the hands and/or feet (for instance, Raynaud's Phenomenon). Most generally understood, peripheral vascular disease includes all related cases of circulatory inadequacy to the extremities.

In addition, in this section, we will report on two other generally related types of problems - thrombophlebitis and varicose veins. Thrombophlebitis is an inflammation of a vein with accompanying blood clot formation within the vein. Varicose veins are dilated, enlarged veins whose valves are damaged. The most common site is the veins of the legs. Both these conditions can be very painful.

Dr. Paul reports as follows concerning his research on varicose veins: "The effect of DMSO on varicose veins was noted inadvertently. The first of the patients in this series, a professional model, had bruised both legs extensively. DMSO was applied to one leg. Within 24 hours, not only had the bruises on that leg nearly completely disappeared, but muscle cramps, which had been present secondary to varicose veins had disappeared in the treated lower extremity. As a result, the patient felt no muscle cramps in the limb to which DMSO had been applied, whereas the other limb continued to show the cramping discomfort as before.

"Following the above experience, 22 patients with varicose veins and associated cramping discomfort were treated. The DMSO was alternated weekly to see if there was any difference noted by the patient in regards to cramping. Twenty-one of the twenty-two patients had either excellent or good results. Moreover, there was a distinct difference noted by these patients when they compared the cramping in the treated and untreated legs.

"In addition to the observation of diminished cramping with DMSO therapy, patients treated for a minimum of eight weeks showed varicosities that were less pronounced, with a definite blanching of the associated telangectasia (small, reddish areas on the skin). There was also a dimunition in associated edema (swelling).

"It was the author's impression that the DMSO seemed not only to reduce the size of the varicosities, but actually to fade the "spiders" which accompany this condition (Paul, 141:593)."

Dosage and Application: The research reports indicate best results are obtained with 70%-90% DMSO applied topically two-four times daily. The amount of each application is one to three teaspoons (5-15 milliliters) of the DMSO solution. Once initial relief and control of the condition is obtained, the frequency of the applications can be greatly reduced - to once or twice weekly.

Application should be to a large, clean area, including and surrounding the specific site of the problem. Once applied, leave it to absorb for 15-30 minutes. Wipe off excess moisture at the end.

Response: Pain relief occurs in 10-20 minutes and lasts four-six hours typically. Treatment period varied from three days to several weeks. Continued improvement of persistent inflammation and the associated complications was recorded for up to three months.

Overall response was best in the early stages of these conditions, more than in chronic and recurrent. Percentage response at the good-to-excellent level ranged from 75%-95%.

QUESTIONS AND ANSWERS

8

What YOU Wanted to Know About DMSO

Can I replace narcotics or barbiturates with DMSO for pain relief?

Many have found that they do receive equivalent or better relief from DMSO. Others find with DMSO they are able to reduce greatly the amount of narcotics or barbiturates they have been taking.

Recent animal studies demonstrated that, in at least some conditions, DMSO works as well as morphine and lasts two to three times longer. DMSO is not addictive.

Have there been any general studies about interactions with other treatments or medications?

Dr. Demos, in the mid-1960's, reported on 1,068 acute and 848 chronic patients with musculoskeletal disorders. "Patients who had been receiving other therapy, such as oral steroids, gold, or analgesics, were instructed to continue that medication." No obvious problems showed up over the limited period of treatment.

Other general studies involving close to 100,000 patients have been reviewed by the FDA professional committees and no significant problematic interactions were noted. Added caution should be exercised, however, with new or long-term medications.

In many cases, the use of analgesics and tranquilizers may be reduced or eliminated when using DMSO. Any changes, of course, should be under the advice and supervision of the prescribing physician.

What about using DMSO with cortisone (cortisol)?

DMSO and cortisone may turn out to be an excellent combination. Hydrocortisone cream is useful for the treatment of DMSO skin irritation. Healing time is the same but discomfort may be reduced.

Several experiments in animals suggest that DMSO greatly (10-1,000 times) enhances the effects of cortisone - at least as an anti-inflammatory.

If you are taking large doses of cortisone or other steroids, you should coordinate any planned DMSO treatments with your physician. Monitor what happens; you may be able to reduce the amount of cortisone needed.

One of the applications by one of the large pharmaceutical firms during the 1960's to the FDA to market DMSO was for a combination of DMSO and cortisone. From what we can gather the test results were quite positive for this combination.

What about mixing DMSO with alcohol?

There are two types of alcohol normally available: rubbing alcohol and drinking alcohol. Neither should be mixed with DMSO. Both will penetrate the skin and more so with DMSO.

Drinking alcohol will gain a better circulation with DMSO, whether taken together or separately. There is a real danger of feeling the effects of drinking alcohol more when using DMSO. Be careful if you intend to be driving.

How long will the breath odor last after an application of DMSO?

There is no hard data on this. It seems to vary with the person. Odor is maximum 2 - 4 hours after application, and greatly decreased after 6 - 8 hours. Most people report noticing the odor up to 12 hours, but a significant number (10% - 20%) report some traces up to 24 hours. Exceptional cases - perhaps as high as 2% - report traces up to 72 hours. All this is consistent with what we know about the breakdown of DMSO in the body.

What is the best way to mask the breath odor?

Nothing really works. Some people feel that wintergreen, spearmint and peppermint are at least helpful. No particular perfume has gained any reputation, although, again, some people feel any perfume is at least somewhat helpful.

What about using DMSO while I am pregnant?

The current amount of evidence on DMSO and possible birth defects is small. We do know that in some extreme cases in animals it can cause birth defects. Without further evidence it would be reasonable to assume DMSO is at least as toxic as drinking alcohol for the fetus. So, if you are planning a pregnancy or become pregnant, stop using DMSO.

It is tempting to use DMSO for lower back pain during pregnancy. But we must really recommend **strongly** that you do not.

A very general precaution that one may choose to adopt is that women of childbearing age should not use DMSO at all. This is really primarily in anticipation of becoming pregnant while you are still using DMSO.

Is there any danger using DMSO if I take birth control pills?

All that can be said for sure is that nothing has turned up in a fairly large incidental sampling. There is no reason to anticipate any problem.

Can I use DMSO around my eyes - for instance, if I have a black eye?

There is no special danger. However, it is a good idea to avoid getting DMSO directly into the eye, unless under the supervision of a physician.

It is conceivable that DMSO might complicate the situation if there is major damage to the eyeball itself.

DMSO has been used experimentally to treat retinitis pigmentosa - a degenerative eye disease leading to blindness. The results were slightly positive. The direct application of DMSO to the eye, under the supervision of an opthalmologist, did not show any special side effects.

Is there any problem in applying DMSO to hairy areas?

No, in general. However, if you use a hair dye or other toxic chemicals in treating or styling your hair, **avoid** using DMSO directly in these areas.

When cleansing the area of intended application, should I use alcohol to sterilize it?

Alcohol sterilization is unnecessary. DMSO will not take bacteria or virus particles through the skin. Also, DMSO is bacteriostatic (stops the growth of many bacteria) at concentrations of 35% or greater.

The "dramatic" ability of DMSO to penetrate the skin and carry other substances with it has been over-emphasized.

Will DMSO bother implants such as plates, pins, artificial hip joints, pacemakers or heart valves?

All these devices are made of materials that are not altered by DMSO. Stainless steel and polyethylene do not dissolve significantly in DMSO at body temperature.

Should DMSO be rubbed in when applying it to the skin?

Rubbing increases the chances of skin irritation for those who are normally sensitive. However, for those who do not find any skin irritation problem, rubbing DMSO into the skin tends to speed the absorption and the effects (by up to 50%). One group reports a generally enhanced response with rubbing: "In some instances the patients found that by vigorously rubbing the site of application, causing a hyperemia (reddened area), this enhanced the rapidity and duration of the response." This was particularly effective in the larger joints and pain sites and in the more chronic types of musculoskeletal disorders.

Why not use DMSO instead of needle injections to introduce substances into the body?

This has been explored, and for some substances it could be used. However, most physicians and patients don't want to wait 30 minutes for the absorption. It is also easier to control the exact amount reaching the deep tissues with either injection or the new occlusive patches.

Is it better to apply heat with DMSO?

Be careful. There is a danger of increasing the chances of skin irritation. Other than that, yes, heat does appear to have an additive effect. Heating pads, sun lamps and so forth are gaining favor among sports trainers.

People with areas of numbness should be extra careful of burning themselves when using heat. DMSO plus heat can increase the danger of burns.

Is it better to apply cold-packs with DMSO?

No. There is no advantage or additive effect. In fact, since the cold may reduce circulation to the area - this is how cold normally reduces swelling - it works against DMSO. DMSO improves circulation to the area and unplugs the clogged microcirculation.

I hurt all over. Should I add DMSO to my bath water?

This won't help. DMSO added to bath water is simply diluted. Instead of increasing benefits you will eliminate them.

DMSO acts both systemically and locally. It acts on the whole body, because it acts on the body chemistry - for instance, like aspirin.

If you hurt all over, just select one or two of the most troubling areas. The DMSO distributes throughout the body in one to two hours.

What about using ultrasonic therapy in combination with DMSO after topical application?

There are some published results on this from the early 1960's. No problems were detected, and none would normally be anticipated. It was reported that when ultrasonic therapy was used immediately after topical application of the DMSO, the response occurred in 10 minutes rather than 20 minutes. It may well speed penetration.

One researcher reported: "In areas where the site of pain was deep- seated, such as in radiculitis or discogenic disease, the use of ultrasonic therapy over the area of application of DMSO was found to speed absorption and hasten response."

Should I apply DMSO just before or just after my shower (or bath)?

Neither. If you shower immediately - up to one half hour - you will wash away much of the DMSO on the skin. If you put DMSO on just after your shower, it penetrates more slowly, like a lower concentration, because there is so much water in your skin from the shower.

The preferable time is at least one half hour before or after a shower or bath.

What about adding DMSO to my normal foot soak?

No. Same problem as above - the DMSO is diluted to the point where it is no longer effective. Greater benefits are experienced from direct application of a 70% DMSO solution. Avoid applying the DMSO at least one half hour before and after a foot bath, shower or swimming.

What about swimming after applying DMSO? Is there danger from chlorine?

There is no significant danger. However, during the first half hour after applying DMSO you would probably wash it out of your skin into the pool.

There is chlorine in virtually all drinking water in large cities, and when swimming in chlorinated pools, some chlorine normally enters through your skin. The amount of increased penetration with DMSO would be insignificant.

Wait one half hour after swimming to apply any DMSO. Right after swimming there is a great deal of water in your skin and this will slow penetration of the DMSO. However, if it is convenient to apply it sooner, there is no added danger.

What about taking DMSO orally?

Dr. Jacobs' Clinic tried this route for many conditions over a period of years. His conclusion is that the ease of administration is not worth the side effects. DMSO reduces stomach acid secretion, thereby inhibiting normal digestive processes with the consequence of gas and/or indigestion.

On the other hand, many of the old "drinkers," as they are affectionately referred to, refuse to change. A teaspoon of DMSO in grape juice at bedtime is still popular.

I heard that DMSO affects the body's immune defense system. Will it increase or decrease my susceptibility to colds, flu or infections?

All clinical trials suggest that there is no significant effect on normal immune defense abilities one way or the other.

In certain abnormal conditions involving auto-immune disorders (where the body's defense system mis-identifies some part of one's own body as foreign and attacks it), DMSO appears to have some positive effects.

What about treating infected wounds?

There are two schools of thought, and very little hard evidence. One group warns of danger of spreading the infection or the toxins produced by the bacteria. The other group mentions improved circulation and that removal of local toxins might help healing.

Since there is no clear and immediate need or advantage to using DMSO on infected wounds, the best advice at the moment is **don't**.

Does DMSO help bee stings?

Don't apply DMSO to bee stings. This is one time when swelling does have a positive purpose. DMSO will reduce the swelling but it may also tend to spread the poison. This is all precautionary, but there seems to be a general consensus that it is best not to do it.

Will DMSO help in the treatment of muscular dystrophy?

No. Of fifteen treatment cases actually reported in the literature, fourteen were clear failures; one might have experienced minor secondary benefits.

What about treating non-infected wounds?

DMSO has been shown to reduce healing time for lacerations, cuts, scrapes and surgical wounds. The amount of scar tissue is also reduced.

Does DMSO work for shingles (herpes zoster)?

The results are mixed. DMSO clearly is not a cure for shingles, but there are numerous reports of symptomatic relief. Relief from the pain of long-term chronic shingles has been reported in a few cases using higher concentrations of DMSO topically.

In Great Britain a combination of DMSO and another agent, IDU, has received approval as a prescriptive medication for shingles. However, DMSO is considered to be a vehicle only, in this combination. IDU has potentially serious side effects which the patient may decide are not worth the risk.

I recently had a heart attack (or stroke). Is there any problem using DMSO immediately or later?

There is no problem, although you should ask your physician about possible drug interactions with any medication you may be taking.

Numerous animal studies over the past 10 years (see the work of Dr. Jack de la Torre in particular) strongly indicate DMSO may be enormously beneficial following (as soon as possible) a heart attack or stroke.

A recent letter to a British medical journal suggested that a patient using DMSO who suffered a minor stroke might have experienced a major stroke if she had not had DMSO in her body.

Formal human trials using DMSO for stroke patients are scheduled to begin in 1982. Heart studies are much further away, unfortunately, because the requisite animal studies have not been completed. But 1981 was an excellent year for DMSO research in related areas, and heart studies are planned.

Does DMSO actually speed the healing process or just appear to?

DMSO does not speed the healing process, but it can reduce the recovery period. By reducing swelling, restoring microcirculation and preventing inflammatory damage, DMSO can remove some of the common inhibitions to normal healing.

In athletic injuries, healing is often retarded by swelling that blocks circulation. A great deal of damage can occur during the first 24 hours after the immediate trauma, due to inadequate circulation and associated inflammation.

Recovery time with DMSO is frequently reported to be half the normal period.

If DMSO relieves stiffness, promotes circulation and prevents damage to tissues, is there any reason to believe that it might be of value in athletic training?

Certainly from what we know about DMSO in the therapeutic setting, it stands to reason that it may be helpful in athletic training. A recent T.V. commercial advertises Ben-Gay as contributing to work-out performance when used at the time of warm-up. DMSO may also be helpful.

(Phil Donahue) "If God didn't want you to swell, he wouldn't make you swell. There is something about swelling that is the natural healing process of the body, and when you correct it, in order to get a highly prized athlete like Daryl Lamonica into Sunday night's game, for which you have just sold 75,000 tickets, we are not sure down the road what kind of long-term physical consequences this may have(?)"

(Sam Bell, Olympic Track & Field Coach) "Every training room in the country uses ice to get rid of swelling - without failure. If you've got something that's more efficient than ice, then why not use it?"

The more we study swelling, the more it appears to be part of the problem rather than part of the solution. Much of the damage of injury occurs **after** the actual trauma.

Will DMSO improve my performance?

This is obviously a touchy question. In some sense, the answer is probably yes, just as Ben-Gay might, by helping to keep you warm.

DMSO is used extensively in horse-racing where the question of drug-enhanced performance is always taken seriously. The jury is still out on this aspect of DMSO.

To our knowledge, there are no studies of changes in grip strength, running speed, endurance and so forth on a controlled, before and after basis, using DMSO.

Since pain is a sign of problems, and DMSO relieves pain, isn't it possible that an injury will be made worse by returning to normal training activity too soon?

There is always the danger of returning to strenuous activity levels before healing is complete. On the other hand, some exercise can often be helpful to healing.

As regards DMSO, it is an analgesic but not an anesthetic. This means that it relieves or reduces pain, but does not eliminate sensation. You can still feel what is happening, most often including some low level of pain. The manner in which DMSO relieves pain is significantly different from narcotics or other analgesics that are also anesthetics - like Novacaine.

Quarterback Daryl Lamonica responds to this question by stating that DMSO doesn't **wipe out** pain and discomfort, it reduces it. You can still tell that it's there. This makes it somewhat less likely that one will abuse a sensitive condition that still needs caution to protect healing tissues.

I heard that DMSO softens connective tissues. Tendons, ligaments and cartilage are composed of connective tissue. Will my tendons or ligaments stretch when I use DMSO?

First of all, DMSO **does not** alter the structure or chemical bonds in normal connective tissue (collagen). The idea that DMSO might lead to structural alterations in normal tendons, ligaments or cartilage is completely without foundation in theory or any clinical experience.

DMSO does alter the metabolism of abnormal connective tissue deposits. This means that the way the body removes abnormal deposits of connective tissue (e.g., scars, etc.) is enhanced by DMSO. It is well-documented that DMSO **does not** alter the metabolism of normal connective tissue.

I run where there is a great deal of air pollution from traffic. Is there a danger if I use DMSO before I run?

There is no increased danger. DMSO does not increase the passage of materials except at the site of local application. Little or no air passes through normal or DMSO-treated skin.

What you absorb through your lungs is hundreds of times more than through either normal or DMSO-treated skin. Having applied DMSO to the skin will not alter the exchange of gases or particle pollutants in your lungs one way or the other.

Recent studies indicate that aerobic exercise in an environment of air pollutants is quite harmful; best to find another place or time to run.

What environmental poisons should I watch out for when using DMSO?

We are aware of only one documented case of poisoning aided by DMSO. Two pesticide researchers in Berkeley, California, were trying various solvents to wash some powerful pesticide off their hands. They tried DMSO and ended up in the hospital for a couple of days.

Pesticides are an obvious danger (with or without DMSO). Paints, bleach, ammonia and hair dye could also be trouble. As a rule, cosmetics and anti-perspirants should be avoided over areas of direct application.

The danger of DMSO-aided penetration of environmental poisons should not be under-estimated, but it should not be over-estimated either. A fairly concentrated episode is needed to pose any real threat.

Is it okay to go out in the sun after applying DMSO? What about suntan lotions?

It is all right to go out in the sun, and there is no problem with any of the standard suntan lotions. Any sunscreen lotion containing Paba as the active agent is all right also. Remember that just about anything that DMSO will take through the skin, will penetrate without DMSO, particularly when left on the skin for some period.

Incidentally, DMSO is an excellent treatment for sunburn.

Why is DMSO so inconsistent? Why doesn't it work for some people?

First, DMSO is no more inconsistent than most other drugs. Differences are often traceable to genetics or metabolism, sometimes to dietary differences. With DMSO it is also likely that many people don't use it properly or long enough to show therapeutic benefit.

Other than that, we can say that the question **is** taken seriously by researchers. It may well turn out to be an important clue as to how DMSO works in other conditions.

The degree of therapeutic inconsistency with DMSO is about the same as is found with aspirin.

Should I discontinue DMSO treatment if local skin irritation occurs?

Unless you are allergic to DMSO, the irritation will **decrease** over time with continued use. You may want to wait a while before another application, and perhaps try a lesser concentration.

In a representative study using DMSO for musculoskeletal problems, an overall 31% of acute injury patients experienced "troubling" side effects. Twenty-five percent continued treatments anyway, but 6% decided to discontinue. In the chronic patients, 35% experienced "troubling" side effects, 30% continued and 5% discontinued.

About 5% - 7% of the populace chooses not to use aspirin because the side effects for them are not worth the actual or possible benefit. This is about the same as for DMSO.

Should I apply DMSO around mealtime?

There is no reason to suspect any interplay between eating time and the topical application of DMSO.